MW01051383

All Scripture references unless otherwise noted are from the King James Version (KJV) of the Holy Bible.

ISBN
9781095404522
For World Wide Distribution

Published May 2019 by She Heals Publishing, LLC
www.Shehealspublishing.com

For other resources or booking
www.authorMarshaScott.com

Introduction

The Secret Is In The Sauce... A 60 Day Journey filled with Passion, Process, and Purpose.

If you've picked up "The Secret Is in the Sauce", it's likely you're someone who is also walking out purpose on your path to your destiny. It is Pastor Marsha's prayer that the information found in this book will encourage and motivate you while you're walking through God's orchestrated events that are sent to help fully mature you into the amazing wife, mother, business woman or leader you are destined to be.

Each day that you wake up to read a devotional found in this book, you will travel through Pastor Marsha's passionate process, and journey towards her destiny. Pastor Marsha often says that she is anointed to tell all of her business, and in this book, she is very transparent in hopes that her readers will find the wisdom, strength and freedom to help them fulfill their destiny. She has a humorous way of letting you behind the curtain of her life to touch her, to see that she is real and become truly inspired that you, too, can overcome any of life's challenges. In her book, she pours out daily doses of encouragement and mother's wit that are sure to inspire and push you into greater!

Table of Contents

Table of Contents

Dedication

This book dedicated to Henry and Judith McGhee (Adoptive Parents), Margaret Brown (Biological Mom), The late Charles and Lillian Scott (In-Loves), Bishop Tony and Lady Celestine Torain (Spiritual Parents), Pastors Thaddeus and Amanda Randolph (Spiritual Parents), all of my Scott Men (Eric Sr., Eric Jr.,Aaron and Darrin Scott), and Musa Agroh (Sister). Also, Apostle Damian Hinton and Pastor Tony Smith for speaking to the gifts within me. Mother Thelma Ramsey and Mother Melody Whitley for mentoring me in intercession. Brown, Jackson, McGhee, and Scott Families (especially Uncle Gary [inside joke], and Aunt Marsha [rest in heaven]). I'd like to especially dedicate this book to my husband and ministry team partner for always seeing the gifts within me, and always pushing me beyond what I thought I could ever accomplish. I thank you from the bottom of my heart for sticking with me through 25+ years of pure process. You are the main ingredient in my special sauce. I love you to life.

Thank You

Whitney Hogans
She Heals Publishing, LLC

Travina Jefferson
Editor

Annie Allen
Graphic Designer

Naaman Brown
Photographer

Nasya Jeffers
Makeup

Kiera Ebb
Image Consultant & Stylist

Ashley Armstead
Lash Tech

Candace Diaz
Forever Diaz Salon & Spa

Ayesha Westmoreland
Allure Hair

Aniecea Thomas
Image Consultant & Stylist

Claudia Johnson
Lafern Design/Event Planner

Shelby Chapman
Personal Assistant

Special thanks to Overseer Eric Scott & Everyone at Lighthouse Worship Center!

Day 1

A Healing Fire

Beloved, think it not strange concerning the fiery trial which is to try you, as though some strange thing happened unto you.
-1 Peter 4:12

Peter admonishes us to not think it strange when a fiery trial or trouble hits our lives. He is making us aware that trials are normal in the life of the believer. I call it the fire of God. When I look back over troubled times in my life, I can clearly see where that particular test burned away some impurity from my life. In Isaiah 6:6-7, the prophet records how an angel touched his lips with a live coal from the fire at the altar, and his sin was purged. God used the fire to burn out impurities within him. I believe the fire is used for the "I just can't help it" situations in our lives. Those problematic areas and situations that we continue to fall into, and then make the familiar excuses such as, "I just can't help myself" or "I just can't seem to stop". Although we don't like the fiery trial, it is true that we emerge from trouble determined not to repeat those mistakes that caused the trouble in the first place. It is not the sin that we want to stop, it's the consequence that we don't want to suffer. Fiery trials can also provide healing. After the hot coal was placed on his mouth, the prophet Isaiah regained a sense of passion and renewed vision. His troubles led to a place of healing and purity that caused him to exclaim, "I WILL GO!". The weight of sin and distraction no longer held him captive and inactive! He was free to go and fulfill his purpose. Don't spend another moment reminiscing on how rough your prior season was. Go forth in the liberation and freedom it produced. Purity comes from the fire, and the purpose that is produced from a purified place will yield a level of productivity that will blow your mind.

DAY 1 PRAYER

Abba Father,
Tests and trials are very difficult, but I thank you because I now
understand that you allow seasons of testing or trouble not to kill me, but
to heal and purify me. I thank you for the divine purifying fire sent in to
my life. It is releasing me to serve you freely. Amen.

LEAN IN

Physical and verbal abuse left me angry as an adult. Anger was always
brewing beneath the surface, however, I never showed it because I
learned to suppress my emotions to survive. Anger would not serve me
professionally, or in ministry. God sent the fire to heal me from
excessive anger by allowing people to mistreat me. This would make me
so angry, but He continued to send one after another until I learned how
to deal with conflict the right way. The Holy Spirit is such an awesome
tutor. God impressed in my spirit that He allowed some things to teach
me proper conflict resolution. The fire or trouble of God can be freeing if
you allow God to do the work in you. I am so grateful to now have
discernment to know when God is at work. This kept me from running
and quitting every time trouble arose. Your fiery situation has purpose,
which just might serve as your healing, so you can operate in greater
purpose.

Day 2

A Kept Woman

Thou wilt keep him in perfect peace, whose mind is stayed on thee:
because he trusteth in thee.
- Isaiah 26:3

Although I am a kept woman, I am not a licensed therapist. I have only avoided Prozac and anxiety medications by the keeping power of God. I've discovered that being kept is a choice. You have a choice to allow your mind to play a full dramatic mini-series filled with potential tragic events that will eventually hit your life, or you can choose to keep your mind on God. Isaiah 26:3 tells us, God will keep you in perfect peace when your mind is focused on him. You may ask, "How do I keep my mind focused on him?" Here are a few things that will help keep your mind on God: continual prayer, meditation on God, studying God's word and keeping positive faith-filled music or words in your ears. There is always something to worry about, but God is offering us a sense of peace that is supernatural. He promised to give us peace that surpasses all understanding. He never said we would live a life without struggles, but with him, we can walk in peace during times of chaos and distress. External pressures of life will arise, but they can't defeat us when our minds and thoughts stay on our God. We are kept by an amazing God!

DAY 2 PRAYER

Abba Father,
You promised to give me peace that surpasses all understanding. This means I can walk around with joy and peace during some of life's most chaotic times. Others will look at me in utter amazement wondering why I haven't lost it. This is the type of peace that I desire to have. Please teach me how to set my affections on things that are above. Oh, to be kept by Jesus! Amen.

LEAN IN

A very close girlfriend once delivered a word from the Lord to me. She told me to protect my peace. I pondered her instructions for a while, but then it hit me. I was a full-grown woman with the right and responsibility to safeguard my peace. God promised me peace, and I would not allow people or circumstances to take that which was rightfully mine. Protecting my peace involved removing toxic people, naysayers and aggravators from my space. I encourage you to do what is necessary to protect your peace. This is not an attempt to treat anyone with anxiety or any other mental health issues. This is more encouragement to those being merely bombarded with the fiery darts of the enemy to take measures to protect your peace.

Day 3

A Treasure Trove

Definition: A treasure trove is a hidden store of valuable or delightful things.

But we have this treasure in earthen vessels, that the excellency of the power may be of God, and not of us.
– 2 Corinthians 4:7

Believe it or not, you are filled with some very valuable things. God placed wonderful gifts inside of you. We live in a society where all the focus and attention is put on external things. As a result, many will spend an extreme amount of time working on the right look, the perfect style and spend countless hours in the gym to have the perfect package. They work tirelessly to improve the external without fully recognizing that they are already filled with gifts and talents that could change the world. If your chief goal is outer beauty, you're aiming way too low. There are countless numbers of pretty women everywhere. Generally, pretty things often get used, discarded and deserted because the person is now looking for something prettier. Sadly, over time, pretty becomes an illusion and gets harder to achieve. Gift cultivation and maxing out on your intellect and learning potential are things that will last, even when pretty has long since gone away. We need to teach our young girls to not only focus on style and glamour, but to also cultivate their gifts. I challenge you to speak to the scientist, teacher, or preacher inside of those whom you lead or influence. I want you to look in the mirror and speak to the author, business owner, and spiritual giant that's lying dormant inside of you. It's time to discover and activate these hidden treasures that lie within. It's in there. It's time to unlock the treasure trove!

DAY 3 PRAYER

Abba Father,
Over time, you have revealed gift after gift that you have placed inside
me. Gifts that I had no idea were on the inside of me. I pray that you do
that for every person who reads this book. Take us on a journey of self-
discovery. Amen.

LEAN IN

This is a real lean in moment. I want you to hear me on this one. You
think you know all the areas in which you are gifted, but you have no
idea the depth of what God has instilled in you. I would've never thought
I'd become an Accountant at 45. I had a fear of math when I was young,
but as it turns out, I have a knack for numbers. I would always say, I'm
a behind-the-scenes person, but here I am on the front line helping my
husband with pastoral ministry. Trust and believe that God has a few
things hidden in you that you have yet to become aware of. Be open and
explore the hidden gifts, talents and treasures inside of you!

Day 4

All My Single Ladies

I charge you, O ye daughters of Jerusalem, by the roes, and by the hinds of the field, that ye stir not up, nor awake my love, till he please.
- Song of Solomon 2:7

When making the list of characteristics and features that you'd like in your future spouse, I'd like to advise you to add one important thing: PURPOSE! It's major! I truly believe this is the one component that has kept me married for 26 years thus far. Lean in and listen. Looks fade. Earning potential grows. Children will become the center attraction. Everything is subject to change except purpose. You were born and given a specific purpose to carry out in your lifetime. So was your future mate. When purpose collides, beautiful and magical things happen. I think we romanticize all the physical components of relationships. Man, the real magic happens within purpose. Feelings come and go. There are times when I feel absolutely in love with my husband. There are also times that I'd love to kick him in his bad knee. However, we've never missed the opportunity to unify as we head out to help a family or counsel a person in trouble. Purpose kept us going when times were hard. We always realized that there was something bigger and greater than us. There are people depending on us to fulfill our kingdom assignment. The enemy has come for us. I believe God warned and protected us because ultimately, He was protecting our purpose. God will give you what you need and some of what you like. Be sure to ask him to give you someone whose purpose compliments yours. For example, a person called to pastoral ministry may not be the best fit for someone who wants to be an airline stewardess spending most of their time in the air and touring foreign countries. They would go in different directions. Purpose is the ticket. Purpose will make your relationship meaningful.

DAY 4 PRAYER

Abba Father,
I believe your people are watching too much reality TV. We've bought into the world's way to secure the perfect romantic future instead of seeking you regarding one of the most important decisions we will make in life. Sober us up. Selection without purpose will provide romantic causalities. Amen.

LEAN IN

We've been romanticized to death. Every channel is showing a romantic love story. We are inundated with romantic connections everywhere. How is it that the romance fizzles so quickly after the start of a relationship? It's because you'll need more than a pretty face, perfect waist or a six pack to keep you vested. When the going gets tough, and it will get tough, you'll need something bigger and stronger than you to pull you forward. It's called purpose. Purpose will make you put your problems to the side to fulfill God's promise for your life and family. I know you think it's all about the lips, hips and finger tips. Keep up with the maintenance of those things, for sure. However, if you want a keeper, ask God for someone with similar purpose in Him.

Day 5

Are You a Sleeping Beauty, Sis?

It is my belief that women are set up from the time they are girls to believe that we need help or rescuing. If you notice in most fairy tales, women are always waiting for the ultimate love of a man. However, the ultimate love, after your love for God, should be your love of self. Please don't overlook who you are today, while waiting for a man to awaken it. You seek out the hidden treasure that God has placed on the inside of you. Everyone is given at least one grace gift. What are you good at doing? What is your special gifting and talent, and how do you go about developing that thing inside of you? I see so many young women discouraged, depressed and in despair while waiting on love. While you're waiting, I would strongly suggest that you discover YOU. Wake up the passion of pursuit inside of you instead of idly waiting around for someone to love you. Look at Leah, Jacob's wife in Genesis chapters 29 and 30. She birthed three sons trying to gain the love, affection and attention of her husband until finally she birthed Judah, which means "praise". When she birthed Judah, something in her awakened to the fact that even if she wasn't loved by her husband, God still loved her. She set her affections on Him. Your praise, in the face of adversity, sends a signal to all that you are a force to be reckoned with. You're not awaiting a kiss from a prince for your awakening either! Kiss yourself! Kiss every unique skill, talent and ability that lie dormant inside of you. Awaken to the possibilities and purpose that await you!

DAY 5 PRAYER

Abba Father,
I now know that I'm more than who I am dating or married to. I'm phenomenal in your sight. You have set times for discovery and development of purpose. My times are in your hands. Please don't let me waste time passionately pursuing love out of season. You make all

things beautiful in your time. Show me if this is a season to focus on you and all the beautiful things you have in store for me. Amen.

LEAN IN

We wait for the rescue. We wait for them to see us, love and help us. This leaves us vulnerable to be victimized repeatedly. Ask God to rescue you. Oftentimes, we invest so much of our time, energy and resources into that significant other, that we fail to sharpen what lie dormant in us. This cycle can go on for years and years, leaving some to never realize their full potential. I am giving you permission to cease being a sleeping beauty. You don't have to live a modern-day fairy tale. Make your own movie. You are the star of the show. Feature and spotlight that awesome grace gift that God put inside of you. You are simply amazing. So, wake up and recognize who you are.

Day 6

Assembly Required

You didn't think you married the total package, did you? Did you think Little Pookie with the beautiful brown eyes would grow up to be the next Barack Obama with little to no required effort? You launched that ministry, built that website and carefully crafted your personal brand with expectations of overnight success. While the effort can be applauded, I feel the need to take you behind the curtains and share a very important ingredient necessary for major success and breakthrough. That important ingredient is called prayer. Greatness is not born, it is BIRTHED. There is some major assembly required to move your situation from the rare or raw talent state, to becoming a functional major operation that God can use. This is where you come in to play. Are you aware of your ability to birth things spiritually through consistent, focused, and disciplined prayer? This type of prayer takes time and focus. Ask God what's in the package, seek out the instructions for assembly and go to work! Piece by piece, prayer by prayer; each declaration of faith, every time you speak the word over your husband, business or dream, you are constructing greatness. My First Lady, Celestine Best Torain, is surrounded by major success in this season of her life. Many applaud and congratulate her on the blessings she's experiencing in this season, but I remember sliding into Thursday night prayer with her. She set the example of diligence in prayer and modeled for me to never come off the prayer wall because prayer produces. People often think greatness is gifted, or that it is just somehow contracted. However, as we cooperate with the manufacturer of the products (people, places and things) that He's entrusted us with, we will see amazing things built up and erected in our lives. It may not seem popular, but I implore you to put in the necessary prayer work, because there is some assembly required.

DAY 6 PRAYER

Abba Father,
Many are disillusioned today from peering over the balcony into the
lives of others wondering why things aren't turning out as great for
them. Father help me to understand that you've provided everything I
need for success and major breakthrough. Grace me with the ability,
patience and fortitude to pray it through. Amen.

LEAN IN

Don't become disillusioned if all you see in front of you is raw materials,
problems, or what appears as a bunch of nothing! What you've been
blessed with is an opportunity to partner with God to birth something
great. Isn't it awesome to know that you'll have a hand in the
development and maturation of an awesome ministry, successful
marriage, booming business or amazing kid that grew up to take the
world by storm?

Day 7

Conquering Depression

As I begin today's devotional, I want to make it clear that I am not a medical doctor. Those who suffer with prolonged bouts of depression are encouraged to seek out the appropriate medical help. With that said, I would like to share a few tips on conquering mild depression that I pulled from a popular bible story found in 1 Kings chapter 19. In this story, the Prophet Elijah found himself exhausted after a great victory over the 450 prophets of Baal. Many times, spiritual warfare and times of being greatly used by God can leave you feeling withdrawn and depleted. If you neglect the necessary self-care, you are left with these early signs of depression. Even though excessive sleeping is also a sign of depression, you don't want to continue to push past exhaustion for the sake of functioning just to survive depression. In 1 Kings 19, God took note of the Elijah's emotional state and prescribed rest and refueling for His prophet. Though we may be powerful spiritual agents, we need time to mend after intense warfare. We really need to take time to care for our physical and emotional needs, and I believe that's why God allowed some time for His prophet to sleep while He prepared his meals for refueling. Jezebel's threat left the prophet so fearful and discouraged, that he vacated his post, went into the wilderness and asked God to end his life there. God identified that this was his exhaustion speaking. He knew that rest, refueling and redirection would help Elijah change his outlook. That prescription can help us as well.

DAY 7 PRAYER

Abba Father,
I know that emotions are needed and necessary, but please help me to manage my emotions. Please help me take the necessary steps to manage them, instead of my emotions managing me. Help me take advantage of your wisdom you gave to Elijah. Amen.

LEAN IN

I have struggled with depression most of my life. Here are a few methods that I use to stay on top of negative emotions:

Think on these things - I keep the word of God in my ear through videos or television.

Reject negative thoughts - I learned that every thought is not a "God thought" or my thought, so I practice casting out those negative thoughts.

Resist the pit - I deal with negative thinking and feelings at the onset. If I allow them to linger, I find myself sinking deeper and deeper in what I call "The Pit." A trip to the pit can leave you stuck in negativity for weeks or longer.

Listen to worship music - It lifts my spirit.

Fellowship - Sometimes church and the saints can be funnier than the local comedy club.

All of these work together to help me conquer depression.

Day 8

Be the Solution

One of my favorite female bible characters is Abigail, found in 1 Samuel 25. Her bible story depicts her as a woman who was married to an out-of-control man, who made foolish decisions. In fact, her husband Nabal's name meant "fool". Are you married to a fool? Is your supervisor a fool? Are your children out of control and making foolish decisions? We all will encounter people who fail to operate in wisdom and lack sobriety, but I recommend that you learn to follow Abigail's example when those times come. She didn't spend a lot of energy addressing the one with the foolish behavior, instead, she went into action to solve the immediate problem she faced. You must become solution minded. How can you use your prayers, unique set of skills, strengths and influence to make things better? You are a problem solver, whether you know it or not. Leaders don't sit around complaining over unfair or unruly circumstances. This takes no brains or creativity. God used Abigail's behavior, when faced with an impossible situation, to upgrade her. Likewise, your solution mindedness and problem-solving abilities will cause you to be noticed and secure your upgrade too. Another notable thing Abigail did was move swiftly in taking leadership and ownership of the situation. Abigail took inventory of the resources available to her, assessed the proper timing to execute her plan, gave directions to her staff, and set her plan into motion. Her decisive actions and quick wit saved her entire household. You are a natural born leader, too. You have the wisdom of God inside of you that is needed to save those that you've been assigned to cover and lead. In the end, her leadership and thoughtful moves caused her to be remembered. Keep leading while bleeding, keep managing the messes in your life, and continue to make the best of bad situations because your skill and creativity will shine through. King David remembered her and came back to make Abigail his wife after hearing of her husband's sudden death. In the end, she was promoted to the position of future queen.

DAY 8 PRAYER

Abba Father,
You've entrusted me with a few messes, and you're using them to develop
my leadership and problem-solving skills. I thank you for taking me
higher and increasing my capacity to handle more money, power, and
ministry. Amen.

LEAN IN

Every problem that you solve makes you shine more and more. They
give you opportunities to use your unique abilities and cause your
brilliance to become more apparent to all. Approach your next
assignment with a mind to dominate. Whatever challenges are presented
to you, know that you were born to handle them. You have the abilities
of God inside of you, and there is nothing that you and God cannot
handle together. Lead on!

Day 9

Brokenness

Anyone that God has used in a major way has gone through what I call a "process of brokenness". For example, let's consider the life of Hannah, found in 1 Samuel, chapter 1. We find Hannah being loved by her husband, Elkana, but grieved because she couldn't have children. Hannah had a sister-wife named Peninnah who was able to bear children while Hannah was left barren. I'm sure it had to be an emotionally, mentally and possibly spiritual breaking to see a person continue to be blessed right in front of you with the very thing that you desire. To add insult to injury, Peninnah pushed Hannah to grief and frustration by continuously acknowledging the obvious fact that she could not produce children. What Hannah did was allowed her brokenness to produce power, fire and life. Her pain pushed her into the temple to pray what is described as a fervent prayer. An effective, fiery prayer of a broken woman will produce much. Your brokenness will produce for you too, if you channel your pain into power. Hannah's prayers produced life; she finally birthed a son. That's what the pain associated with brokenness is designed to do. It should cause you to bear down and travail. What does it mean to travail? It's that serious prayer. You know the prayer you pray when you are experiencing trouble? It's not that quick five-minute prayer for safety that you say on your way out the door each morning. It's focused, postured prayer. Through her travailing, focused and postured prayer, Hannah eventually birthed life. She named him Samuel, and he was a GREAT prophet. Can you look past your brokenness to see what power, fire and life you are supposed to birth? God's plan for your brokenness is to usher you to your knees to ask Him for help. Why? Because you don't have the power to produce greatness on your own. Just imagine the kinds of prayers, service, prophecies, witty inventions or gifts that will flow out of your broken vessel. However, I'd like to look at two other facets of brokenness: continued brokenness and brokenness of release. After Hannah gave birth to Samuel, her brokenness resumes when she had to give her son to the priest to fulfill the promise she made to the Lord. I am sure that it hurt to release her dreams. That very thing she yearned and prayed for night and day. There will be times in your life when you too will feel the brokenness of release. God will require you to let go of what you had in mind for your marriage, career, or ministry; brokenness ensures that obedience is cultivated within us. Unfortunate circumstances that break you also provide you with an opportunity to surrender and do things God's way again and again. When these circumstances hit your life, they break your routine and your peace. Over time, these disruptions cause pain and eventually numbness. Then you find yourself still, broken before the Lord, and depending on His mercy to simply keep your mind from minute to minute. What happens during these times that produce power, fire and life? There is a pressing for your very survival that lands you in the very lap of God. You're not seeking His face; you're seeking His lap where He consoles and comforts you in your brokenness. This level of intimacy with God, even though you are broken, causes you to emerge with a clarity and empathy that you may not have known to exist before. You now feel the need of that young single mom, because you once took a huge financial hit before. Now you do more than see her need, you take action to meet her need. Since you've experienced infidelity in a relationship, you invite that young couple over that's struggling with infidelity to try and facilitate healing through prayer and counseling. You understand the devastation of infidelity and you really want to help someone else navigate those troubled waters. Your time of brokenness will not only cause you to stop screening your calls, but it will inspire you to make the calls to release a word of wisdom or encouragement. Since you've cried from the lap of God for him to hold you together, you're more effective, sensitive and powerful as a vessel that's broken but very useful to God.

DAY 9 PRAYER

Abba Father,
Help me to move through the pain of my circumstances. Help me to rise,
although numb and without answers, to do the work you put into my
hands to do. I throw myself on your mercy, knowing that help is on the
way. I also know that I am the help that someone is depending on, so

please help me push past the pain and allow the oil of the anointing to flow out of me to help meet their needs. Amen.

LEAN IN

I respectfully asked God why the rejection, why the abandonment, and why the childhood abuse? Why such a long, arduous process to emotional healing and wholeness? Why was I so screwed up to the point that I needed so much processing and attention? I paused, reflected and cried a deep cry while writing this one. I didn't want these life experiences, and I'm sure Hannah didn't want her pain either. I didn't get a long drawn out answer, but I did hear that my brokenness and processing will help others. Also, I heard," I WILL REPAY". All I could do was sit in the local deli near my home and weep. I let you behind my curtain today. We see people's glory, but we don't always know their story. Their personal sacrifice or level of brokenness is required for them to do what they do. I sat with my face in my hands in that deli, and I began to thank God for deeming me worthy of helping others. I want to flow in power, fire and produce life.

Day 10

Dealing with Disappointment

My soul, wait thou only upon God; for my expectation is from him.
-Psalms 62:5

People are prone to disappoint you! Family, co-workers, and friends will let you down. Why? Because even with the best intentions, people are limited and only have a certain capacity to perform for you. If you approach an individual expecting them to give you everything you need, to always show up for you and make the difference in the matters concerning you, it's a set up for disappointment. No one person has everything that you need. So, to go into a friendship, marriage, or business relationship with unrealistic expectations is not recommended at all. I can remember asking my pastor for the church keys and going down to the empty church. I laid before the Lord on a cold, ceramic floor after experiencing a huge let down from people that I love. God whispered Psalms 62:5 ever so sweetly in my ear. I immediately went over to one of the pews and picked up a bible to read that scripture. When I saw that it said my EXPECTATION should be from God and not man, honey, I left that church with a whole new lease on life! No more tears. No more looking to man to do for me what my God already had in mind to do for me. Disappointment is difficult and painful. If you don't allow God to sit upon the throne of your life while you look to Him for provision of all that you need, it's very possible to end up a bitter, angry person. It could possibly put you on the edge of a nervous breakdown. I live by that scripture now. I'll never forgot that day at the church, and now my expectation is rooted in God. He is the author and finisher of my faith. His love for us is amazing, and He will never let us down. He is absolutely in our corner, especially during times of major disappointment.

DAY 10 PRAYER

Abba Father,
I look to the hills from which cometh my help, because all my help comes
from you. Help me to continue to look up to you, because I know in my
heart that there is no failure in you. Amen.

LEAN IN

I have counseled many people who despised their own life because
another person let them down, cheated on them, or walked away. I can
relate because I have suffered major disappointment with people, but I'm
so glad that God totally revolutionized my thinking with one scripture. I
personally think God allows people to disappoint us because He wants us
to learn the importance of coming to Him in all things. He is Abba
Father, and we can rush into His loving arms any day at any time for the
love and comfort we need. As you maneuver through your life, please
proceed with caution. Misplaced expectations could possibly cause a fall
that you can't recover from. Reserve your hopes and dreams for the one
who can make them a reality.

Day 11

Don't Fight to Defend! Fight to Win!

The thief cometh not, but for the steal, and to kill, and to destroy; I am come that they might have life, and that they might have it more abundantly.
-John 10:10

We've all heard the term "cat fight". It is typically depicted as two women swinging aimlessly at one another in a windmill fashion with their eyes closed, barely hitting the mark. When we picture two men in a fight, they're in a good boxing stance with their feet squared, hands up and ready to go throw blows. Well, in Ephesians 6, we learn that we are engaged in spiritual warfare. Let's establish this truth: you absolutely have an adversary in which you must contend. I don't care how much you try to dismiss the idea or ignore him; he's coming whether you send for him or not. Our adversary is relentless, and there is no reasoning with him. When I was less spiritually mature, I can remember purposely backing off my spiritual assignment in hopes that the enemy's activity would come to a halt. I was weak spiritually and couldn't handle what was coming at me. So, I reasoned that if I stopped, the devil would stop too. This was not the case at all. According to the Bible, our enemy's mission is to steal, kill and destroy, but Jesus' mission is to destroy the works of the enemy. So, there are two opposing sides at work, but it's good to know that Jesus is on the winning side! Now that you're on Jesus' side, you've been given spiritual authority, so don't waste time swinging at the wind. You're not fighting to defend; you're fighting to win. You can't close your eyes, make a wish and hope that you land a few blows. You must be a thinking fighter. You will need a God-strategy, and you'll find that in prayer, praise and worship. He'll show you how to defeat every adverse situation that comes in your life to halt, hurt or hinder you or your family. Once God gives you the battle strategy, show no mercy. Execute every detail. If God tells you that it will take forgiveness to secure victory, forgive! If He instructs you to walk in unconditional love, love! He may instruct you to remove yourself from a toxic situation. Whatever it is, fight to win!

DAY 11 PRAYER

Abba Father,
Your word admonishes me to give thanks unto to God who gives me the victory and causes me to triumph! I stand on your word. I will fight to win! Please give me the strategies that I need to come out on top, and the spiritual intelligence needed to protect and cover my family. Amen.

LEAN IN

You can fight to defend or fight to win. What's the difference? When you fight to defend, you're fighting just to show up every day, hold the marriage together or keep the business afloat. You'll get tired of just merely surviving. Fighting to win involves seeking the face of God. When you leave the presence of God, you emerge with fresh strategy and blue print plans designed to force the enemy out. You now have spiritual ammunition! Your landing blows are breaking down the enemy's schemes and devices. You must mature in your ability to fight. When you get sick and tired of being punched in the mouth, like me, eventually you will get mad enough to rise in prayer, fasting and worship. Do whatever it takes to win!

Day 12

Don't Mess with Sarai

You may have powerful people in your life who do not treat you well, or with the respect you deserve. They can leave you feeling like you're at the mercy of their opinions and actions toward you. You are not powerless, nor helpless. I'd like to share one of my favorite bible stories from Genesis 12 that speaks to this. During biblical times, if a king saw a beautiful woman that he wanted to add to his harem, he would simply kill the husband and take her for himself. Abram was aware of this, and when confronted by the king to inquire about his relation to his wife, Sarai, Abram lied and said that Sarai was his sister. He sold her out to save his own life. Sarai had no real power to speak up or defend herself. When faced with abusive or unfair situations, remember that God sees and will protect you when people fail you. God will speak up for you when you can't speak for yourself. Sarai should've been able to look to Abram for strength and covering, but he was fearful and weak during this important moment of their lives. Who is it that should've stood up for you, protected and covered you, but turned out to be weak? Here's the thing, a person can have the best intentions, but like Abram, have areas of weakness. Psalm 62:5 tells us to wait and trust in God, and that our expectation should be in God, and God alone. There is no failure in Him! God sees you and knows how to handle your abuser to stop the unfair treatment. God sent a plague to the house of the king who took Sarai to warn him not to touch her. God has a way of letting those who intend to harm you know not to mishandle you. God took extreme measure to ensure Sarai's safety, and he will do the same for you because he is our powerful protector.

DAY 12 PRAYER

Abba Father,
You're the one who numbers the strands of hair on our heads. That's how in tune and in touch you are with your children. It is light work for you to handle those who abuse power, as it concerns your children, so

I'm trusting you to fight for me. I know you will win because you are the greatest power, and you shall not be defeated. Amen.

LEAN IN

I have watched a couple of former supervisors get escorted off jobs by security. They were fired from their positions after constantly abusing the power that came with their jobs. I've never prayed for the downfall of those in authority, I simply cried out to God when their misuse of authority began to affect me negatively. I've learned not to waste time trying to fight my own battle, win wars with words or prove I'm right in matters. When folks relentlessly come for me, I go to God in prayer. Also, I have learned to pity them, because I know they are headed for a Holy Ghost intervention on my behalf. I have learned to pray for my enemies, while waiting patiently for God to deal with my enemies. He hasn't failed me yet, and I know he won't let you down either. You may be dealing with a verbally abusive spouse, toxic relative or crazy co-worker. Stop fighting in the natural and access the power of prayer. Laying down your weapons will allow God to start fighting on your behalf.

DAY 13

Don't You Worry Your Pretty Little Head

*Lift up your heads, O ye gates; and be ye lift up, ye everlasting doors;
and the King of glory shall come in.*
-Psalm 24:7

One of the weapons of the enemy is to attack the believer with slander. Since he can't stop you from walking through an open door, he will often try to silence your voice and influence with a demonically influenced smear campaign. It's even worse when Christian brothers and sisters lack discernment and participate in the enemy's cruel campaign. I've fallen victim to this type of attack, and it's a very painful thing to walk through. One of the greatest lessons I learned during an attack is that you must walk through it! When you go through this type of attack, you will be tempted to track down the source of it. I am telling you, don't do it! Regardless of who he is using, please know that Satan is the source. His plan is to slow or shut down your progress with your kingdom assignment. You'll even have times when you feel like it's not even worth trying to fulfill your assignment because you probably won't be well received due to the enemy's smear campaign. Just keep moving! There's only one thing you can do with a rumor, and that is to out-live it. Over time, your consistency and anointed behavior will overshadow the lies that were told. I always say you can argue with me, but you can't argue with the anointing. It is God's stamp of approval. Psalm 24:7 tells us, *"Lift up your heads, O ye gates; and be ye lift up, ye everlasting doors; and the King of glory shall come in"*. So, you can lift your head and heavy heart, because the King of Glory is coming to vouch for and validate you in the face of the enemy. God is coming to nullify his smear campaign. All you need to do is show up and be anointed.

DAY 13 PRAYER

Abba Father,
Thank you for using the hurt and pressure of verbal attacks to deliver us
from the opinions of people. I now understand that the attacks are a
major part of our spiritual development. I ask you now for the grace to
walk with our heads high in you. Amen.

LEAN IN

There was a young girl in the book of Acts, chapter 16, who followed the
men of God shouting a truth. The problem is, she did it with the wrong
spirit and motive. I've had times when people have taken a small truth
and magnified it as large as they could in attempts to destroy me. You
might ask, why would anyone want to destroy me? They are motivated
by jealousy, envy or covetousness. Slander can deal such a major blow
and leave you wounded. The key is to fall into the arms of your loving
Abba Father who will stitch you up, grow you up, and then oil you up
(anoint you). God opens new doors, grants new friends and won't allow
the enemy to halt one opportunity. It's His process of vindication. Hang
in there!

Day 14

Refuse to Die a Victim!

Be sober, be vigilant; because your adversary the devil, as a roaring lion, walketh about, seeking whom he may devour.
-1 Peter 5:8

In 1 Peter 5:8, we are taught that our adversary, the devil roams around as a roaring lion seeking whom he may devour. In truth, we live in a fallen world where bad things often happen to good people - God's people. It has been my observation that the enemy first sets out to daze you, oftentimes through divorce, adultery, bullying, body image issues leading to low self-esteem, abuse, job loss, or even bankruptcy. These types of traumas left unchecked or without support will have you reeling your whole life. Victims will often find themselves moving from one bad situation to the next without ever gaining composure or the proper footing. Just one major blow from the enemy through childhood trauma, or in your adult life can leave you feeling out of control for the rest of your life. It can leave you open to being victimized again and again. The enemy of your soul is relentless, and it is usually during these times that addictions (sexual, substance and financial, etc.) are born. We rock, reel and spin trying to cope, totally unaware of the fact the enemy is behind the scenes orchestrating a well thought out plan to make you die a victim.

For example, divorce can leave one bitter, angry, consumed and unable to love again. Childhood trauma, due to molestation may leave the victim feeling powerless and having a lack of control throughout their life. Childhood bullying can have a lasting impact on a person's confidence and self-image. This can lead to bad relationship choices and possibly cause them to look for love in all the wrong places and can lead them to substance abuse as they try to numb the pain.

I believe that one of the primary ministries of the Christian believer should be to help the victim, even if that victim is yourself. Instead of trying to convince others to come to our church just to increase church membership or meet a quota, we should seek to use our gifts to help people overcome in the areas that they have been victimized. How can we empower them in the areas that they have been broken? What if you used your prophetic gift specifically to speak to that area in another that is totally broken? We may have been a victim, but it is not God's desire that we die a victim. He is the potter, and He desires to assemble broken places and spaces inside us and others. Jeremiah 18:4 assures us that when the potter saw that the vessel became flawed and injured, he used that same clay and made it into another vessel that seemed good to him.

DAY 14 PRAYER

Abba Father,
Reach down your powerful hand to steady me after the enemy's attempt to sabotage my life. Place my heart, mind and hands in a position to fight for recovery and strength so I can stop the cycles of victimization. I declare and decree that I am no longer the victim. Please help me minister this same truth to someone else who may have been victimized, so they won't die a victim. Amen.

LEAN IN

My mom committed suicide when I was 19 years old. As a result, I dealt with some early childhood trauma. Satan was counting on my countless bad choices to lead me to the same fate, but God, with His supreme power stepped in to stop the cycle. The goal of my transparency and ministry is to stop the cycle of victimization in the lives of others. It is not always comfortable to share my mistakes and missteps, but I share them to warn, educate, and interrupt the plan of Satan. There are far too many people stumbling from one devastating event to another without our intervention. I do understand that many cases require licensed professionals but let us not stand by, apathetic and un-engaged, because many cases simply require our anointing to keep someone else from dying a victim.

Day 15

Everything that Glitters is not Gold!

People watchers often experience needless pain, so, I'd like to offer them some advice. My advice is to not believe the hype. What hype? Social media hype. Many spend hours scrolling on the various social media platforms that are available. They view what they perceive to be countless numbers of couples in love, living a glamorous life filled with relational bliss, and appear to have no problems at all. Here's what happens after all the scrolling, they find themselves depressed and coveting what seems impossible for them to ever attain. If you find that scrolling for hours watching the lifestyles of others leaves you depressed, I suggest that you limit yourself or stop scrolling for a while. I have personally watched a few of the millennials that I mentor do this very thing. I must remind them that everything that glitters is not gold. I encourage them to spend less time on social media and begin working to build their own glamorous life. However, I tell them it is so important to wait patiently on God for their next, their increase, and even that future husband who's designed just for them. I encourage you to do the same as things aren't always as they appear, and you don't want to end up wasting valuable years headed in the wrong direction. As Christians, it's so important that we develop Godly contentment as we live our lives in front of the world. Just as we're guilty of watching people, people are watching us as well. We're not attempting to show a fake "us", but a faith filled "us" who truly believes God has our next in mind. We don't have to grab, scratch and claw to make our next our now. In Philippians 4:11, the Apostle Paul stated that he'd learned to be content in whatever state he found himself, and that's the model we should be attempting to follow. I really believe that shifting our focus, time and energy towards our own personal journeys will aid in our being content. Resist the urge to compare your journey with someone else's. God wants to give you a life that others can behold!

DAY 15 PRAYER

Abba Father,
Many of us are suffering because we watch the lives of others, then begin
to compare and compete. Please heal our discontentment. Reassure us
that what you have for us is for us. It's just a matter of time before we
walk into our own manifested blessings. Amen.

LEAN IN

One of the things I have stopped doing, as I age, is making comparisons. I have learned to stay in my own lane and try hard to run my own race. I refuse to peep into the lives of other female ministers, churches or co-workers to compare. As soon as you start focusing on what others are achieving or attaining, you lose joy in what God is doing for you. Social media often facilitates unintentional, and sometimes innocent prolonged peeping and comparing. Another problem with comparing and sacrificing your own joy, is that the people you secretly stalk have their own share of problems you know nothing about. Use your energy to work on overcoming and being content while attaining your own personal victories.

Day 16

Experience Freedom

Many churches begin the top of the year with some type of a fast to offer God the first fruits of the new year. One year, I had a dream that members of our church were lining up for miracles and I was instructed by God in the dream to go on a year-long fast. So, I obeyed. I proclaimed that the year would be the year of miracles! God taught me something on my year-long journey. One of the greatest miracles that one can receive is the gift of freedom. In Isaiah 58, we see that God chose that particular fast to loose the bands of wickedness, and to let the oppressed go free. I would rather be free from anxiety, fear and depression, than get a new sports car. Material things don't equate to peace, joy and happiness. During my fast that year, I watched God intentionally orchestrate things in people's lives to free them from the opinions of people, toxic relationships and even bad habits such as overspending. There were others who fasted with me for short periods, who wanted the release of specific things like a loving husband, new job or much needed financial blessing. Amazingly, I watched God orchestrate things so that those same people were free to enjoy the mate as well as material and financial blessings at the appropriate time. God makes everything beautiful in His time. There is nothing more beautiful than experiencing the liberating power of God. Finally, I want to encourage you with the fact that God is getting ready to free up and release that thing you have requested through prayer and fasting.

DAY 16 PRAYER

Abba Father,
I thank you for the work that you've done within me. I am free to love myself and others. I am free to forgive. I am free from the deceptive lies of the enemy that constantly bombard me with thoughts that I am not good enough. I appreciate your wisdom and timing. You knew not to release certain things to me before it was time. Amen.

LEAN IN

Fasting is a tool that I wish I'd employed when I first received Christ. There are some things God will do for us, but there are some things we must do for ourselves. Matthew 6:16 opens with, *"when you fast"*, which implies that there is an expectation that we should be living fasted lives. If I could leave you with one piece of wisdom today, it would be to make fasting a regular part of your life. Fasting will change the game and revolutionize the way you live. Fasting frees things up. You can spend less time waiting and wondering, and more time enjoying the freedom and joy of the Lord.

Day 17

Extended Reach

I believe some people come into our lives with the express assignment to offend us. As much as they are fulling their assignment, if we fall for the bait, we'll stop operating in love. Galatians 5:6 tells us that faith works by love, and consequently, without love, we stop our faith from working effectively. Refuse being baited into quarrels, conflict and unnecessary drama whenever possible. Did you know that you can choose to forgive folks before the offense even happens? I have grown in my faith and love walk, and I believe you can too. When I learned that being in offense could possibly, or ultimately shut down or limit the flow of blessing into my life, I decided that was too much power to give to other people because they were not worth it. This is a discipline that can be developed, but it's a choice. Take the infraction to God in prayer, immediately. Make up your mind that you will not spend the next 30 days to a year in offense. Instead, continue to secure every blessing God has for you by responding in love. Know that your proper response is going to be the vehicle to extend your reach to the unseen realm, and cause blessings to find you right where you are operating in God's love and forgiveness.

DAY 17 PRAYER

Abba Father,
You told us to forgive our brother seven times seventy. We ask for your grace to forgive an offense at the onset. We realize this is something that we cannot do in our own strength. We know that it will take time to forgive, but we are committed to the process. Amen.

LEAN IN

You are faithful to your ministry, sowing seed and committed in every way. Yet, you cannot figure out why things aren't moving and flowing. This was my experience for many years until I learned this principle.

My faith is very much connected to my love walk. I did not have the type of faith that could move mountains because I had teaspoon love. I don't even think it was a whole teaspoon. When my faith and love began to match, I saw God move quite a few mountains in my life. Check out your agape today. Are you loving unconditionally?

Day 18

Faith Forward

Now faith is the substance of things hoped for, the evidence of things not seen.
-Hebrews 11:1

Faith Forward is a term that dropped into my spirit after my husband was diagnosed with what the doctors were calling an incurable auto-immune disease. Amyloidosis is such a rare disease that I had to Google it to find out its meaning. My life became super overwhelmed after his diagnosis. We had to see several specialists for possible treatment options, which was emotionally draining. Then, I was left alone to manage the responsibilities of what should've been a challenging two-person team at work after a co-worker resigned. If that wasn't enough, I had to assist my husband with pastoral duties because we believe that every individual needs and deserves pastoral covering. It was one of those "Everywhere you turn, it's something else" times in life. We all have them; you go to work, there's issues. You come home, more issues. Even at church, there's a fire to be put out or problem to solve. How did I make it? Faith Forward is what God dropped in my spirit! I would tell myself to move Faith Forward every chance I had. I would not allow myself to consult with my feelings or agree with my circumstances. I don't care how grim the diagnosis or heavy the workload, it was always Faith Forward. I only allowed myself to think on what the Word said about my situation, and what God said to me prophetically in the past year! I meditated on the things the Lord spoke to me concerning my future. This, dear-heart is why you need a Pastor. You need the logos and rhema word spoken into your life regularly. Since I'd heard it preached by my Pastor, I took Hebrews 10:38 where it says, *"The just shall live by their faith"* literally, and this is what I did daily! I told myself, you don't have time to cry or die, you must keep moving Faith Forward! Now, here we are four years later, and God has done miraculous things. He will do the same for you, but you must learn to walk by faith and not by sight. Hebrews 11:1 says, *"Now faith is the substance of things hoped for, the evidence of things not seen"*. Keep moving Faith Forward!

DAY 18 PRAYER

Abba Father,
I pray for those that are dealing with health challenges and other overwhelming circumstances. Healing is the children's bread. You won't put more on us than we are able to bear. Increase our faith. Take us from faith to faith! It is by your stripes that we are healed. We receive it. Amen.

LEAN IN

I felt like I was holding everybody up. I didn't want my children, my church or family to see me fall under the weight of my circumstance. I felt that if I fell apart, everyone else would fall apart too. This may or may not have been true, however, it's how I felt at the time. I am thankful for everything that God took me through preceding my husband's diagnosis. It all prepared me to stand. I was stretched in ways that you could not imagine. If I can offer some advice at this moment, I would say don't consult with your feelings. Consult with the words of God. Look to his written, preached and prophetic word! It will keep you moving FAITH FORWARD!

Day 19

Favored, Fierce, Flawed... Facts!

A man's gift maketh room for him, and bringeth him before great men.
-Proverbs 18:16

I recently did a workshop with the ladies at my church. I shared with them that their gifts are designed to get them into the room and a seat at the table. It will serve to give them an audience with great people, as Proverbs 18:16 promises. I encouraged them to believe that people are already in position, waiting to take them to the next level. We also discussed that it is essential to be just as aware of your flaws as you are your gifts. Why? Flaws, by definition, are imperfections or weaknesses that detract from the whole and can hinder effectiveness. In other words, your flaws can hinder you from ever making it into the room. If you have a bad reputation that precedes you, it can shut doors that God intended to open. People may say "she's gifted, but her attitude is terrible" or "she's challenging to work with". Flaws can also get you kicked out of the room. You can work your whole life towards a specific goal. Your hard work pays off, and you finally obtain the dream job or mate. However, your failure to be confident to own all of you, flaws and all, can introduce unnecessary complications that can affect your next. You must be brave enough to dig deep enough to assess both trash and treasure on the inside. What is it about me that is not serving or helping me? What do I need to excavate? You must keep it real with yourself and ask yourself questions like: What are my character flaws? Am I prideful or a little messy? Has gossip or unprofessional behaviors such as chronic lateness caused me to miss out on opportunities in the past? Dig deep, and to your own self, be true. While it's important to cultivate those gifts, it's equally important to challenge yourself to work on your imperfections, as well. As favored and fierce as we may be, as 2 Corinthians 4:7 reminds us, those treasures are still housed in a flawed human vessel.

DAY 19 PRAYER

Abba Father,
I need confidence and discernment. I need the ability to face and
recognize all of my features and imperfections. Bless me with the ability
to see clearly the areas in which I need to cultivate as well as what to
work on, so I can be my best self. Amen.

LEAN IN

During the workshop, I gave all the ladies little buckets with shovels
attached. The buckets were filled with all types of delightful things. They
were instructed to write down one flaw, fold the paper, and place it at the
bottom of the bucket. The analogy came to show them that they are filled
with wonderful things, and they are a true delight. However, despite all
the wonderful things inside of us, we must be aware that everything
about us in not wonderful. I encouraged them to sift through the
greatness to become self-aware. Your flaw can hinder the flow of what
God has in store for you, so don't get stuck at an impasse. Remember,
you are favored, fierce and flawed. Now, that's a fact!

Day 20

Forfeited Harvest? I think not!
Dedicated to Overseer Eric Charles Scott Sr.

Genesis 8:22 teaches us, *"While the earth remains, seedtime and harvest, and cold and heat, and summer and winter, and day and night shall not cease"*. Now, if a person planted a seed in a flower pot, then proceeded to stand over the pot, day in and day out to watch for growth, we would say that person was strange. I don't want you to be called strange. God promised that the harvest will always follow the seed, so we don't have to stand over it waiting for the harvest to appear, it's going to take some time. Just as it is in the natural, it will take time and care before you see the fruit of your spiritual labor. My husband taught a lesson entitled, "The War of the Wait". In his teaching, he explained that there is real warfare involved while waiting for what you have sown to manifest. Because the warfare is mainly in your mind, you began to wonder if the time and energy that you've invested in your ministry, relationship, child or business idea will ever yield a harvest. I want to remind you that we walk by faith, and not by sight, so if you've sowed, you must believe that you will reap a harvest. What the adversary does is make sure that the areas in which you have sown paint a picture that speaks lack of appreciation, barrenness, and disappointment. Why? Because he wants you to stop sowing and walk away disillusioned having never obtained a return on your investment. Here is another twist to this teaching, you will not always reap in the area that you've energetically and faithfully sown. For example, I could have spent years working in the nursery at the church while the children that I taught about Jesus may not have a whole lot to give back to me, but I don't worry because I'm just sowing my seed and expecting a harvest someday. Fast forward ten to fifteen years later, my son receives a full ride scholarship to the University of his choosing. Many would miss a miraculous yield of seeding and reaping because they don't see the two as connecting. What if I quit working with the children because I felt it wasn't a visible position that merited acknowledgment or appreciation? Don't worry, you will also reap in the area that you have sown. God makes sure that your investment yields a harvest over time so that you don't quit. Remember there is always seed, time, and then harvest. You will reap your harvest of blessing in your appointed season if you don't faint and forfeit it.

DAY 20 PRAYER

Abba Father,
Thank you for giving seed to the sower. Give me the strength and grace to continue to sow despite the lack of evidence concerning my harvest, adverse conditions, or the amount of time that I must wait for my harvest to be manifested. Amen.

LEAN IN

My husband and I served as pastors faithfully for 12 years, and out of nowhere, ministry blessings began to come our way. My husband teaches that there are five seasons: Winter, Spring, Summer, Fall and DUE season. Don't miss your due season because of impatience or discouragement. Your efforts will eventually pay off, but remember, it typically gets the hardest right before your breakthrough. Hang in there. Don't quit. Forfeited Harvest? I don't think so!

Day 21

God is Preparing Me

I am reminded of an old Daryl Coley song entitled, "He's Preparing Me". Some of the lyrics include great lines such as: "God is preparing me for things that I can't handle right now", and "He's providing me with what I need to carry out the next matter in my life". Then the lyrics go on to say; "God is preparing me because He cares for me, he's preparing me for everything that comes in my life".

Psalm 84:7, the voice translation says, *"They journey from place to place, gaining strength along the way; until they meet God in Zion".* I truly believe we go from strength to strength and grow from our experiences as we journey through life. I can remember going to visit my biological mom and younger sister when I was a teenager. My biological mother was dealing with the effects of longtime substance abuse, and although not diagnosed, I believe some mental health issues as well. During one visit, she got into the bath tub fully dressed and began to wash and scrub herself. She cried a lot during that visit while she was attempting to communicate how sorry she was for giving me away at 3 months old. I remember not really knowing how to process what was going on, and I had no idea how to help her. This visit left me confused and in tears. Many similar visits left me crying but producing no tears; I was all cried out. I didn't realize at the time that God was strengthening and conditioning me so that I could stand under the weight of future chaotic situations. Pastoral ministry requires that I not only remain strong under the weight of my family and personal problems, but I also have to bear the weight of others while God is taking them to a place of healing. Four years ago, my husband was diagnosed with what doctors are calling an incurable auto-immune disease. He has undergone ten painful throat surgeries so far. I'm only able to be strong for him, my family and our ministry because of prior conditioning that took place in the middle of chaos and pain. Athletes continue to train during their off season to maintain and build their endurance level. However, God is the master trainer! He orchestrates situations in life to teach you how to persevere. This is a part of your spiritual training, so do not despise it. God is making you a spiritual giant. He's making you a person that He can trust to be strong under the pressure of ministry and success. You may have times where you're all cried out, but it's just conditioning you for greater.

DAY 21 PRAYER

Abba Father,
You are the master teacher, trainer and coach. You have success and prosperity in store for your people. Help us to truly embrace the fact that it does not come without cost. Just like we take much time and care to prepare our children for their next levels of learning, you are the ultimate parent, and you are getting us ready for things up the road that we are not currently prepared to handle right now. Amen.

LEAN IN

I stopped to have a real good ugly cry as I concluded writing this passage today. I am remembering Margaret Brown. She was my biological mother. I was blessed to have two mothers. I thank Margaret for choosing to have me when she could have opted to have an abortion. She also had the wisdom to allow me to be raised occasionally by another family that was in a better position to parent me. I celebrate her for her courage. I remember her humor, toughness, and ability to fry to best fish I've ever had! She'll always have a special place in my heart. I am strong now due to the things that I've experienced in life. God has taken me from strength to strength. He's doing the same for you!

Day 22

God will Anoint YOU!

Many of us have taken severe blows to our self-image and self-esteem, but we must be very careful not to begin to emulate others and eventually take on this false sense of self while attempting to escape us by being them. It's a very strange and often painful thing to watch a person lay down their personality, voice tone, and individual style to be somebody that they admire or may feel that they're better than them. This looks like a person with a more subdued, laid back personality who suddenly turns into a bubbly cheerleader right on cue. Or, a fiery evangelist who will suddenly turn off the fire to morph into a Senior Pastor/Shepherd in hopes of obtaining a certain status or place in the eyes of specific individuals. In reality, it will take almost a lifetime for some to find and come to terms with who God created, called and anointed them to be. It could take a lifetime to fulfill that call with confidence and excellence. So, please do not waste another day attempting to operate in someone else's anointing and calling but stand on the word in Psalm 138:8 where God promises to perfect that which concerns you. Besides, Ephesians 4:16 teaches us that we are the body of Christ, fitly joined together, supplying what the other needs. If you are trying to be me, you can't provide what I may need from you. Take a moment to think on this harsh truth; you can't use your gifts, personality and uniqueness to be a blessing in someone else's life if you don't learn to embrace, own and love who you were created and anointed to be.

DAY 22 PRAYER

Abba Father,
You talked to us about the works of the flesh, through your word. Please help me not to operate in emulations, because I now understand that this is a total disrespect to you as my creator. I don't want to appear as if I'm telling you that what you created is not good enough. Forgive me and help me to walk in my own unique talents and abilities. Amen.

LEAN IN

I do not struggle with emulations. I tend not to do a lot of comparing, either, because I've discovered that comparison is the thief of joy. If you spend a lot of time studying and copying what you find attractive in another person, it will leave you feeling sad and inadequate. I choose to focus on the full-time job of being the best I can be, while cultivating and developing my own unique gifts. You need to get to work as well! We do not need another carbon copy, we need a designer's original!

Day 23

Godfidence

One of God's greatest gifts to me is, what I call, "Godfidence". Godfidence is what's gained after allowing God to process you to the point that you look to Him for affirmation, and you no longer depend on people for constant approval. This process you walk through helps you become aware of the fact that even though it's you who is operating and flowing in the God-given gifts that God has given you, it's His supernatural power and anointing that makes the difference in your effectiveness. This process of becoming Godfident was one of the most grueling experiences I've ever had to endure. There were many times during the process where I thought I would die, and I did, I died to Marsha. I believe that God allows circumstances to break us down only to build us back up, but better. You might ask, "What do you mean?" There are so many factors in our lives that have helped mold and shape our identities, personalities, and outlook on life. The person we have become doesn't necessarily reflect the image of Christ, so the demolition and reconstruction begin. He excavates the things that are not like Him, such as self-aggrandizement, bad attitudes, and immature behaviors that do not reflect our better selves. It is a painful process to be made aware of the things that are in you, that are not serving you, and to have to cooperate with God while He's changing you. I didn't like it and you won't either, but it's necessary. God, in turn, will go on to add the things in us that may be lacking like courage, strength, and wisdom. I call this being on the Potter's wheel. Around and around we go, but we'll emerge from the wheel as new, confident women declaring like the Apostle Paul In Galatians 2:20, "I am crucified with Christ: nevertheless, I live; yet not I, but Christ lives in me". Be ready to step into the plans and purposes of God, full of Godfidence.

DAY 23 PRAYER

Abba Father,
I need to have my confidence rooted and grounded in you. This will
make me unshakable and unstoppable. Help me to endure whatever
process it takes for me to be molded and shaped into your image. Amen.

LEAN IN

Listen! I thought I was going to die. I had so many things wrong with
me, but Holy Spirit and I began to partner together to make me over. I
thought He was going to throw the young woman away and start again,
but we discovered that I had many wonderful features, gifts and talents
that He intended to use. This did not negate the fact that I had many
areas that needed God's touch. I am thankful that I was able to gain
understanding that this is how God works. If not, I would've gotten
discouraged and walked away from God. I don't want you to be
discouraged, because I am a living witness that you will walk in more
freedom and Godfidence than you can imagine if you stay the course and
endure the process. You will radiate true Godfidence!

Day 24

How to Swim Among Sharks

Everybody is not going to like you. Everybody is not for you! Everybody does not want to see you win in life! Big Facts! You are a kingdom woman that walks among those that are not necessarily kingdom citizens. Everyone that attends church is not in church, if you know what I mean. The Bible warns that there will be tares, goats and wolves among us. So how do you navigate the fake? How do you out maneuver the snake? How do you manipulate around the pits and traps that have been set for you? Honestly, I am still learning. One thing I have established is that you better have a real relationship with God. You will be hurt and disappointed by people in your family, church and work environment. It's inevitable. They represent danger in the waters of your life and it could be for several reasons. You can't get out of the water. You can't quit life. You can't avoid going to work. You must learn to be flexible and fluid. It is true when a person shows you who they are, you should believe them. I suggest you take it one step further. Before engaging, ask God to show you who they are and believe Him. Fools rush in! We are Kingdom! We love! I am issuing a warning. Love with discernment! Proverbs 4:23 warns us to Guard our heart with all diligence! What does this mean? Allow God to love through you. He'll show you where to invest. He'll show you who to invest yourself into. Everything must be done at God's leading. Too many times we put ourselves out there naively. We don't move at the voice and command of God. We suffer deep lasting hurt. The type of hurt that is debilitating and interrupts purpose. We can't remove the sharks from the water. We must learn to coexist. We must occupy the same space as our predators, haters, people that want to see us choke. I tell my mentees, "Everyone has somebody who wants to see them choke." Predators Prey! It's what they do! You can make up your mind that they won't be given the opportunity to prey on you. Determine that you will not be their lunch. Set up healthy boundaries. Ask God who's real and who's really for you. Listen, to me. It will save you a lot of time and headache.

DAY 24 PRAYER

Abba Father,
There will be false and fake everywhere we go in life. We ask that you
show us the gold plated, counterfeits and knock offs that enter our lives.
Amen.

LEAN IN

I did not grow up in church. I didn't truly understand the culture. When
God saved me, I dropped my hoodie at the foyer of the church and
proceeded in with my rose-colored, stylish glasses. Wow! I was in for
rude awakening! I thought everyone was somehow connected and
related to Jesus. NOT! The hurt and pain that I experienced due to my
naivety cannot be captured in this short paragraph, so I won't attempt to
explain. Here's the thing, I recovered! I also made it out with some
wisdom to share with you. GUARD YOUR HEART! Ask God about
each person you encounter. Work with them, serve them, but only let
them in IF God tells you to. I am trying to save you some time and
energy. Listen to me, don't you allow folks to have access to you unless
God tells you to.

Day 25

Humility Option

Humble yourselves therefore under the mighty hand of God, that he may exalt you in due time.
-1 Peter 5:6

1 Peter 5:6 teaches us that if you humble yourself before God, He'll lift you up. However, the opposite is true as well. If you lift yourself up, God will take you down a peg or two. I have experienced both scenarios and now I choose humility. I choose to give God the glory in all things. What does this mean? It simply means giving God the credit. It's coming to the realization and acknowledgment that it was God who gave you all your unique gifts, talents, and abilities. He also affords opportunities to cultivate and showcase them. We don't have to walk around with a false sense of humility with our head and arms hanging to the ground refusing to take a compliment. That's not godly humility. God wants you to be confident and godly proud of your achievements, while appropriating the credit back to him, showing that you realize He is your source. The Apostle Paul was given the ability to see spiritual mysteries, but he was also given a thorn in his flesh to ensure he didn't get the big head because he'd been given so much. Have you been given a whole lot of intelligence, artistic ability, graceful speaking ability or beautiful looks, but find yourself being poked with trouble from time to time? That's God! You just may have been assigned a thorn to keep you level headed. Let me share a tip with you, the more you work on staying humble, the less you'll get poked. I choose the humble option. The scripture tells us to humble ourselves, which suggest that it's our responsibility to develop the habit of deferring the glory and credit to God. If we don't, we will experience the poke that none of us want to experience. This type of pain is a reminder to give credit where credit is due.

DAY 25 PRAYER

Abba Father,
I thank you for your built-in system of ensuring I stay humble and
gracious, regardless of how much I am given, or how high I'm blessed to
go. I know an inflated ego will hinder my potential and pride will
eventually cause me unnecessary pain. Amen.

LEAN IN

I struggled with pride at one point. I felt that I could just do, go, quit and
say what I wanted when I wanted, but God loved me enough to use some
situations to teach me some valuable lessons. He was showing me that
he was more than just my Savior, but He is Master, Ruler and Lord of
my life. We are to humble ourselves under His mighty hand by living
our lives on His terms. I've come to realize after seasons of being poked
by strategically placed thorns, to do things God's way and in God's
timing.

Day 26

I Would Like to Meet You

But we have this treasure in earthen vessels, that the excellency of the power may be of God, and not of us.
-2 Corinthians 4:7

Shame is a piece of emotional baggage that we can't travel with. We need to work to rid ourselves of it. Secrets and lies internalized generally lead to shame. Many have beautiful personalities, assets and features hiding under a cloak of shame that others need to experience. 2 Corinthians 4:7 tells us that treasure can be hidden in earthen vessels. You have awesome spiritual gifts, or hidden treasures inside of you that God wants to identify, unlock and unleash. He cannot bring them out into open view due to the cloak of shame. Did you ever have a feature like an overbite, being the shortest kid in the group, or maybe the skinniest one in the neighborhood that was the source ridicule? These are all things that can leave a person to grapple with shame. Even with all the possible past trauma you may have suffered at the hands of rude and inconsiderate peers, the reality is that you are too unique, too gifted, and too powerful to be covered by a cloak of shame. So, I'm calling you out from that cloak of shame because you will one day speak your truth, even if the only person you can reveal your secrets to is Jesus. Isaiah 9:6 teaches us that He is our Counselor, and I believe speaking your truth to your counselor will make you free. I thought at one point that I was shy, but I am not shy. I may be introverted, but not shy. I was grappling with that cloak of shame. I was scared to speak up. I was soft spoken and scared to look people in the eye. Someone projected their perversion on to me through abuse. After what I survived, my abuser should have been ashamed, not me, but I was. Thank God for the Holy Spirit helping me to look up, speak up and come out from underneath a false self that had developed right under my nose. Because the Holy Spirit helped me to get free from shame, I know and believe that with His help, you too can be free from shame. I look forward to experiencing and meeting the real you, with all your beautiful features and assets uncovered by your maker. I want to watch you flourish in your true identity and authenticity.

DAY 26 PRAYER

Abba Father,
I thank you for removing the cloak of shame from me. For years, I didn't even realize it was there. I appreciate you being a safe place to tell my real story. You are indeed a wonderful counselor. Amen.

LEAN IN

God began to show me that I have the gift of exhortation, but this involved communication. How could this be when I am so shy? What I called shy was a cloak of shame brought on by an experience in my early childhood. I was forced to keep it a secret, and to live a lie. I internalized the lie which brought about shame. Today, as I share my truth, I am free from the shame of it all. I'd like to see you free from shame too. I am so excited about meeting the real you!

Day 27

I'll Never Tell

I struggled with whether to talk about molestation. Today, the thought came to me, how can you write a book to build women and not address the best kept secret in many of their lives. Well, I have a secret that I want to tell you about. I was molested by more than one person as a child. I tried not to keep it a secret, but I grew up in a time when things like inappropriate touching or fondling were not talked about. If you did bring up the subject, it was quickly dismissed or swept under the rug. What we will readily talk about are the after effects of the abuse and the victim's destructive behavior, resulting from such abuse. You hear the older women say, "she's fast", or "he's just wild". There is often much to be shared about a young woman or young man that we observe engaging in too much of whatever behaviors they are exhibiting, but where is the discussion to discover what may have caused this excessive behavior? If we are going to be effective in ministry, we must get down to the root of the matter. We may not be licensed therapists but getting to the root may prompt you to help a person who is in need to seek a therapist. I am 49 years old and my environment is still not totally safe for me talk about the abuse I suffered. Although one of my abusers is dead, I knew if I shared my story, I would be viciously verbally attacked. I understand why those that are abused don't tell. Our society is set up to protect the abuser more than the victim. Many young women and men are left to try and work out what happened to them on their own. What we see are symptoms of what ails them that gets acted out through their coping mechanism of choice. Therefore, I feel compelled to share my story. In reality, we hear so many stories of abuse that we've become numb to it, and we want people to get over it already. We have no time to deal with it, after all, we have ministry to do. It could be just as simple as allowing a person to tell their truth and providing resources for them to get the follow up they need. We are called to help those that have been hurt by abuse, of any kind, to heal and to lead them on a path to wholeness. If the spirit of Christ truly rests upon us, we'll find ourselves administering help and healing everywhere we go.

DAY 27 PRAYER

Abba Father,
I thank you that you can be touched by the feelings of our infirmities.
You care for every person reading this prayer. Please meet each one us
at the point of our need, especially if one of us has had to harbor secrets
of abuse. Also, please give us wisdom to aid those that may have
suffered abuse of any kind. Amen.

LEAN IN

Christ has healed and made me whole from the trauma of verbal, physical and sexual abuse. He took me on a journey that ends at age 49. 7 x 7 = 49. Seven is the number of completion, and I've been blessed to finally complete seven cycles of completion. Now, I can share my story from a place of victory. God used me to encourage and assist others on their path to healing. I truly believe God has entrusted many of us with experience because He knew He could use our mouths, hands, and hearts to help others heal.

Important Note: Child sexual abuse is far more prevalent than most people realize. It is likely the most prevalent health problem children face with the most serious array of consequences. About 1 in 9 girls and 1 in 53 boys will be sexually abused before they turn 18[1]. This year, there will be Thousands of babies born in the U.S. that will become victims of child sexual abuse UNLESS we do something about it.

1. The Lifetime Prevalence of Child Sexual Abuse and Sexual Assault Assessed in Late Adolescence, 55 Journal of Adolescence Health 329, 329-333 (2014), as cited by RAINN.Org

Day 28

It's A Celebration!

But I say unto you, love your enemies, bless them that curse you, do good to them that hate you, and pray for them which despitefully use you, and persecute you.
- Matthew 5:44

God tests the righteous! One of the most difficult tests to pass is receiving an invite to the launch party of your enemies. In Matthew 5:44, God instructs us to love and pray for our enemies, but what happens when He requires us to watch them walk into their blessing? We think that because we're mad or done with someone that God should be done with them too. No, God loves your haters too. You feel like God must be on your side, right? God is always on the side of what's right. God is not on either side and is patiently waiting for both conflicting parties to grow up. A part of our growth is having to witness the elevation and blessing of those that have opposed us. This will not be accomplished by the spiritually immature or those who have not died to self. So now you're being required to attend a celebration that you thought would be a vindication. I've dealt with this agape test recently. I set myself to rejoice with my enemies, and I earnestly prayed for grace to truly be happy for them in their time of promotion and celebration. God was faithful to release that grace and help me pass the test. There is a grace for you too. You will be stretched to become bigger, to be more Christ-like, and to walk out the gospel that you so boldly proclaim, preach and teach. I believe there is real spiritual power released to those who walk in extraordinary love. I wonder how many forfeit designated blessings because they walked in sloppy agape. Don't let that be you! Develop the love muscles. You'll be able to stand up under the weight of the major blessing and promotion that's sure to come your way.

DAY 28 PRAYER

Abba Father,
I know that you will stretch me, and you will require me to love the way
that you love. I know that you don't require me to hang out with my
enemies, but you do desire that I'm genuinely happy when you choose to
extend mercy and grace to them. Please give me the grace to fulfill your
will in this area. Amen.

LEAN IN

I recently bypassed sickness, my own personal grief, and exhaustion to
attend the launch party for someone who'd previously hurt me deeply.
The hurt was never acknowledged. Neither was an apology ever offered,
but I set myself to walk in love and forgiveness as God instructed. The
night of the launch, I received an offer to minister at a major event. God
ministered Psalm 17 to me the next day as He assured me that I was the
apple of his eye. God has a way of letting you know when He's pleased
with your response. He lets you know when you've met the
requirements and passed the agape test. All that week, I received call
after call extending free items that I needed personally. It may feel like
people are getting by or are getting over on you, but God keeps score.
When you respond correctly, He repays you in such a special way that
you know it's Him. Continue in mature Christ-like behavior, He'll make
sure that you have many reasons to celebrate!

Day 29

It's Possible to Miss Out!

We are often encouraged to name it and claim it, blab it and grab it, or just decree a thing! Such proclamations often have us feeling like we can't lose. The reality is that disobedience, a bad attitude and other bad behavior will cause you to suffer losses. Such is the case with Queen Vashti in the book of Esther. She was summoned to appear before King Ahasuerus, during his seven-day feast. On the seventh day, when the heart of the king was merry with wine, he commanded that Queen Vashti be brought before him, wearing her royal crown to show her beauty to the people and officials. Queen Vashti refused to come at the king's command. I've heard this story taught and preached many different ways. It was suggested that Queen Vashti had a valid reason not to appear before the King, but whatever the reason, she ended up being replaced and lost her prominent place in the kingdom. I can remember periods of frustration in marriage, ministry and on the job where I wanted to defy those in authority. In my mind, I had adequate and sufficient cause to rebel and do my own thing. Honestly, sometimes I did exactly that, my own thing. God taught me a principle; life is not always fair. People in leadership positions are not always right. However, if we are assigned to a person, we do not have the option to confront, rebel or walk away. You must swallow your words while waiting for God to work on your behalf. I've had to bite my tongue, humble myself and endure some things to serve God, while serving His people. I always believed in serving God while serving His people. My goal is to always work to bring excellence to situations that were not always good to me. I strive to give it my absolute best, although, I do not always get it right at first. God has honored me through promotion by fixing the situation. Other times, he made a way for a new situation, but the key is, you must allow God to lead you in each case. No one likes to be the recipient of unfair treatment. David endured unfair treatment by King Saul, Joseph endured unfair treatment by his brothers, and Hannah also endured unfair treatment by Peninnah. All three received a major promotion and major blessings. It is imperative that you learn to be still even under the most challenging situations. A wrong move due to impatience or lack of submission can leave you crown-less and replaced.

DAY 29 PRAYER

Abba Father,
You told us that those who live godly will have trouble and suffer
persecution. I thank you in advance for long suffering and the spirit to
endure such cases. I thank you for the grace to continue until you make
your will clear to me. Amen.

LEAN IN

I had my bags packed. I was out of here. I wasn't going to take mistreatment another day. I told myself, I don't have to take this crappy treatment. Who do they think they are? Touch not God's anointed! I had scriptures to back up my immature behavior. I was young at the time and hadn't grown up spiritually. Spiritual growth came after I ducked a few javelins and was thrown into a few pits. I also experienced my share of Peninnah's who vexed my entire life. The reality is we need a few imperfect experiences in life to shape our spiritual character. If not, we'll grow up to be obnoxious spiritual brats. I tell myself often, "Marsha, eat that! It's for your good. God has a purpose in it". I remind myself that God vindicates, but He also replaces. I try to keep a good attitude in suffering, so I don't miss out.

Day 30

Judge your Aunt Sophie

Are we judgmental? Did you know that in whatever measure you judge someone you will be judged by others? Matthew 7: 1-5 teaches against judging each other. I believe if we truly understood that we will reap what we sow, we would be more cognizant of the thoughts we think and words we speak. The next time you receive harsh criticism or hear your name in the rumor mill, ask yourself if you were recently unforgiving to another. I have found myself mid-turmoil and realizing in that moment that I'd sown judgement. The Holy Spirit would whisper to me that I was reaping judgement. Yikes! It's a hard thing to admit that you brought negativity on yourself, but with this realization you are destined for a reaping season. It won't be pleasant, and you won't be able to wish or pray it away. You'll have to walk out the same condemnation, lack of mercy and impatience you heaped upon another. I suggest that you acknowledge your wrong quickly. The Holy Spirit will lead you into all truth, even the truth about yourself. Throw yourself upon the mercy of the court. Ask God to forgive you and cut your reaping season short. I think God allows us to reap negatively to teach us empathy. Without empathy, we can possibly find ourselves judging people's behavior without knowing any of the circumstances that led them to behave in that manner. Be careful, because God knows how to give us a taste of what we're judging. He'll give us just enough of an experience to make us want out, and to look for a path away from the seat of judgement.

DAY 30 PRAYER

Abba Father,
We are not to judge unless we want to be judged. Forgive me for my critical nature. You alone are the righteous judge. Help me to view people in the light that you see them. They are redeemable and have great worth. Amen.

LEAN IN

I judged a person once, who had hurt me deeply, and called them a demon. I really did. I felt they were being used by the devil, so they must actually be the devil. All jokes aside, I took the position that there was just no hope for them. So, I did not pray for them because I felt they were a bad seed. God taught me through a few hard trials to never see his children as bad, even when bad was being done to me. We are instructed to love and pray for others. We stand in the place of God when we judge others. I learned a valuable lesson and a hard truth; leave the judging up to God.

Day 31

Just Get Over It! NOT!

One of my pet peeves is for a person to tell another person to simply get over the hurt caused by another person. We often quote a random scripture on forgiveness as if the admonishment to walk out the word of God is done without much effort. Forgiveness is a process, and depending on what the offense was, it could take longer than what you may expect. The key to healing and recovering from hurt is to first acknowledge that you are hurt, then immediately take your hurt to the Lord in prayer. You'll be tempted to talk about what happened to you but keeping the story line on repeat will only serve to increase your pain level and prolong your healing. I am not implying that you can't talk to a trusted friend or advisor, because Proverbs 11:14 tells us that there is safety in Godly counsel, but I am suggesting that you don't continue to rehearse your story to everyone that will listen. It's like picking at a scab every time you see it; it will never heal. I grew to the place that I could take deep hurt to the Lord in prayer and leave it there. This ability came after I handled hurt the wrong way, which left me angry and bitter. I found that this state will not only leave you ineffective, but people will shift, and God will lift. Nobody wants to be around an angry, bitter person. I know you may feel justified in your feelings and actions, but unforgiveness will only hurt you, while the people who perpetrated the hurt are happy, free and could care less that you are hurting. So, choose to forgive, even without the acknowledgment of wrong doing or an apology. Your winning strategy is to meditate on scriptures pertaining to forgiveness, and depending on how deep the wounding, you may also have to fast. It will be worth the effort when you can be free to love and live an abundant life free from unforgiveness.

DAY 31 PRAYER

Abba Father,
Forgive them for they know not what they do. Please give me the
strength to pray for and love my enemies. Help me to realize that

releasing those that hurt me releases you to deal with them according to what their deeds deserve. Amen.

LEAN IN

I struggled with unforgiveness for years. I felt justified holding grudges against those that hurt me. Somehow, I felt like forgiving them was letting them off the hook for the mean-spirited things they did to me. This is when God began to teach me that I was locked in my own spiritual prison, and a root of bitterness was lodged in my soul. I gained a lot of weight, my personality changed, and I struggled with depression. It was awful. God was merciful to uproot the bitterness and teach me how to pray for those that hurt me so deeply. Please understand that those were some dry, monotone prayers at first. As I kept at God's principles, I was able to not only pray for them, but learn to love many who purposely did me wrong. When we obey God, even when we don't feel it, He gives us grace to forgive. I'd like to add that some cases were so difficult that I needed to go on a Daniel fast because I know that fasting releases. The good news is that God will vindicate you, so choose forgiveness, it's God's way! In His time, He will help you to get over it.

Day 32

Keep Throwing That Gift

A man's gift maketh room for him, and bringeth him before great men.
- Proverbs 18:16

In Genesis 37, Joseph had a dream that he would be placed in a high leadership role, even above his parents. He was severely rebuked after sharing this God-given dream with his family. His jealous brothers set in motion a series of events, which ultimately separated Joseph from his family. He was isolated, but his gift of dreams, and the interpretation of dreams was fully intact. Joseph used (threw) his gift, even after his brothers sold him into slavery, and he ended up in a prominent position within Potiphar's house. Joseph's bonus gift of biceps, triceps and beauty landed him in prison after being falsely accused by Potiphar's wife. If we are honest, we might look at Joseph and say that he had the reasoning to become discouraged and bitter and could have then placed his gift on the shelf. On the contrary, Joseph chose to continue to throw his gift no matter what situation he found himself in. After interpreting two more dreams, Joseph's gift eventually freed him from prison, and he was promoted to the highest place of prominence, second to the Pharaoh. If you chose faithful service to God over bitterness, you too will eventually transition into a higher place of purpose. Proverbs 18:16 assures us that our gifts will make room for us and bring us before great men.

DAY 32 PRAYER

Abba Father,
Please help me to realize the power of what you placed inside me. Help me to not lay my gift aside after experiencing rejection, deceit or betrayal. My gift came from you, so please help me to always throw it back in service to you. Amen.

LEAN IN

It is your gift that will get you in the door. You will need to have a strong determination to continue to use it regardless of whether it is celebrated, appreciated or rejected. I show God my appreciation for his grace and mercy by giving my gift back to Him. I use my gifts in service to Him. I'll continue to throw my gift back to the Master because He is worthy of excellent and faithful service. I will give it back to the one who unconditionally loves and forgives me. So, take your focus off people and remember who gave you the gift. God did. Be determined to give Him your all. Continue to cultivate that gift, and God will see to it that room is made for you.

Day 33

Let's Talk About It

What is prayer? Prayer is simply a conversation with God. However, I think when we use weighty terms like "Prayer Warrior" and "Intercessor", we can unintentionally discourage people from the prayer experience altogether. It's as if we unknowingly make the prayer experience only applicable to a select few, but prayer consists of amazing conversations that we all have with God throughout the duration of our Christian experience. Another great component of prayer is that you can talk to God in the way you communicate. You don't have to drop your voice down a few octaves, nor shout at the top of your voice. God hears you just the way you speak normally. God desires that you talk to him about everything, because He takes delight in you. In fact, Zephaniah 3:17 teaches us that The Lord your God rejoices over you in singing. Now that my sons are all off to college and other pursuits, I love hearing from them and look forward to moments that open for us to chat. Although God already knows what's going on in your life, He wants you to ask him for what you need. He wants you to express your fears, worries and concerns, and He will answer you back with what you need. I don't want you to wait for a booming voice to thunder from the clouds, but God will impress answers down in your spirit. He may answer through nature or your favorite television show. His answer may come immediately, or it may come over time. Just know that when you reach out to Him, look for, and expect Him to reach back. It's a privilege, and an honor to be able to come boldly to the throne of grace. Don't fear approaching Him because you didn't do everything right. Confess your faults to God and believe that He is faithful and just to hear and forgive you. Start a conversation with God today, He wants to talk about it!

DAY 33 PRAYER

Abba Father,
Teach me the accessibility and ease of prayer. I thank you that I don't
have to travel through life alone, but I can talk to you anywhere, and at
any time. You are a God that never slumbers nor sleeps, and you delight
in hearing from me, engaging me and ultimately blessing me. Amen.

LEAN IN

I would get up at my appointed prayer time, go into the living room,
which was my prayer place, so I wouldn't wake hubby, and sit on the
couch. I would sit there, numb, feeling too exhausted to pray. I believe
God would interpret my silence, but I knew enough to get up, and go to
the appointed place to communicate to God that I knew there was no
failure in Him. You see, my husband had recently been diagnosed with a
rare auto-immune disease. I was worn out from many doctor visits and
the emotions associated with the recent diagnosis. One day I ran across a
video of my sons singing beside my husband's hospital bed, and the
words led me to the throne. I was able to move from how I felt, to a
prayer posture. I didn't have a powerful, prolific prayer. All I had was
my heart, my words and my personality. I started the conversation, and
in His typical, faithful fashion, my God answered back. You should start
a few conversations concerning the matters on your heart today. God is
saying, "Let's talk about it."

Day 34

Lies, Longevity and Lace-fronts

There is nothing like a good comeback story. I recently watched the testimony of one of Christendom's finest. She entered a bad abusive marriage at the start of her ministry. It was publicly humiliating for her. She seemed to persevere through it. I watched her ministry gain momentum over the years. She never stopped ministering the gospel. She's still very relevant in Kingdom to this day. Today, I saw her advertisement for her beauty line. The enemy is strategic to smack you early at the onset of purpose. He's hoping to publicly embarrass or humiliate you into stopping. He uses lies and deception to make you think that you can't overcome one of his attacks or mistakes you've made. Don't believe the hype. Rahab was a woman in Joshua, chapter 2 who had a past. She made a good choice that led her to a future that included being named in the lineage of Christ. All you must do is continue to make one good choice after another. You may have to do it in the face of the naysayers or folks who don't want to allow you to overcome your past. Keep choosing what's right again and again. Before you know it, you'll have your own business, new boo or new ministry platform.

DAY 34 PRAYER

Abba Father,
Help me to forgive myself and choose what's right. That's all. Amen.

LEAN IN

I am always rooting for the underdog. Your setback is an opportunity for a comeback. You can learn from your mistakes, regroup and begin again. It all starts with one right choice. There's turnaround and prosperity in your future!

Day 35

Love Letter

God is dealing with me about writing a love letter, but I am not sure who to address. Should I pen a letter to God expressing my appreciation for all that He's done for me? How about my husband of 26 years, or my three fellas? I feel the strangest inclination to write a love letter to myself. Where do I start? Do I even love myself? Can I even find the words to express what I feel about me, to inspire me? I am left scratching my head and patting my weave. Like you, I focus primarily on staying humble, grounded and avoiding self-aggrandizement so much that I forget to focus on, cultivate and appreciate the qualities about myself that are worth adoration. Do you know that you have qualities about you that God adores? When you look at your child, grandchild or godchild, don't you simply adore them? Even a sneeze or mispronounced word is the cutest thing to you. Similarly, this is how God feels about you. He is not in heaven with a red pen waiting to check off the slightest bit of imperfection you exhibit. Although we go to church regularly, we don't hear too often that God is pleased with and takes pleasure in us. It seems a little strange to some, but God really loves you, and He wants you to love you too. Take a day to reflect on the things about you that you love and appreciate, then wrap your mind around the fact that God looks favorably on those things too. It could be something as simple as the sound of your voice, or the way you notice the needs of others that most would overlook. God made us beautiful...our own special kind of beautiful. For many of us, the enemy has been successful in creating an environment that often causes us to doubt and devalue ourselves, but it's important for you to know that God loves and values you. You are loved, so make sure you love yourself. Block out the lies that tell you that God is not totally into you, amazed by you, and in love with you.

DAY 35 PRAYER

Abba Father,
As your word tells me in 1 John 4:8, you are love! Help me to
comprehend and embrace that truth. Please help me embrace the love
you have for me. Help me to throw away the red pin used to mark all my
flaws, shortcomings and imperfections. Amen.

LEAN IN

I have a spiritual scar that I must work to overcome. At times, it makes me feel like I am less than others, spiritually. But God continues to reassure me that I am more than enough, as He uses me for His glory. He indeed has put His stamp of approval upon my life. I choose not to listen to the voice of my naysayers, and I rise above the contentious looks of those that would make me feel like I don't deserve a seat at the table. I remind myself of the qualities God gave me that are unique, loving and kind. I don't allow my deficits to disqualify me either. 2 Corinthians 12:10 encourages me that it is in my weakness that I am strong through Jesus Christ. There's a lot to love within me, and there's a lot of love in you as well. So, get to writing baby. Write yourself a love letter, put it in a safe place and read it as you need it. Make it a sonnet to encourage your heart.

Day 36

Marriage 101

Today, I am going to provide several suggestions to help keep your marriage healthy. These are things that my husband and I employed over the years. There is no perfect relationship, although there are healthy enjoyable marital relationships. Here are five vital tips to consider:

Tip #1 - Do not attempt to change your spouse. Any change that you force by using anger or any other form of manipulation will only be short lived and leave you frustrated. Prayer is the key to lasting change. You'll have to exhibit patience while waiting for God to do the internal work within your mate. God renews the mind. The heart of the king is in the Lord's hands. He will turn your husband's heart towards you. He'll make him pay attention to the things that matter to you. If you focus on your mate instead of looking to the Lord, you'll find yourself being a nag and argumentative. You can be right but going about things the wrong way. Remember, God designed your husband. He has a great purpose in mind for him. He is more invested in bringing the best out of your spouse than you are. Partner with God through prayer. Take the hurt, pain and disillusionment you feel into your prayer closet. This is the role of the help meet. God will in return give you a marriage that is better than you could ever imagine.

Tip #2 - Remain close friends. I am a firm believer that if partners keep the friendship in place, there are some things that you just won't do to each other. We focus so much on keeping the passion in place while letting go of the basic care and understanding we initially had for one another. Many couples are friends turned enemies. They compete and blame. You started out wanting to see your partner win. What happened? I don't care how angry or upset I may have been with my husband, I never let it stop me from showing up for him. I learned how to tuck our issues, walk by faith, all the while trusting God to fix whatever needed to be fixed. I continued with purpose. I continued to be his friend even at times I didn't really like him. God showed up every single time. If you show up to help your friend complete purpose, God will show up to help you fight every battle. Yes, the enemy came for my marriage over the years, but purpose sent him packing.

Tip #3 - Understand that your spouse will have weaknesses, whether it's his spending habits, a wandering eye or being a workaholic. Everyone is flawed. Everyone struggles with something. I know many may be appalled that I mentioned "wandering eye". I've observed a lot while helping and counseling couples over the last 20 years. I keep my writings 100%. You will need to assess where your struggle lies and that of your spouse and plan accordingly. Superman knew his weakness. I highly recommend that you don't live like an ostrich with his head in the sand and face yours. Be prepared for the enemy and the inner me.

Tip #4 - Never ever let go of date night. You'll need a set time where you allow no interruptions, so you can go away to look in each other's eyes. This should be a separate time from discussing bills or tackling major problems. This should be a fun, romantic or relaxing time. It would be amazing if it were all three. In the early years, we would earmark funds for a stay-cation at a local hotel. I am writing this devotional during one of those stays. We are here celebrating year 26. You must make it a regular practice to get away to refresh your relationship.

Tip #5 - KEEP PEOPLE OUT OF YOUR BUSINESS. I REPEAT. KEEP FOLKS OUT OF YOUR MARRIAGE!

DAY 36 PRAYER

Abba Father,
Marriage is reflective of your relationship with the church. This means that the adversary is coming for marriages. Protect us. Prepare us. Position us to defeat every attack aimed at landing us in divorce court. Amen.

LEAN IN

ENJOYING your spouse? We don't want to stop enjoying each other. We make things so serious sometimes. In our attempts to do ministry, raise children, and build careers, we forget that our spouse used to be our best friend and biggest fan. I suggest getting back to the basics. Getting back to each other!

Day 37

Met in Motion

Life is not an event; it is a journey. I recently listened to an interview where the statement was made, "I gave up many times, but I did not quit", there couldn't be a truer statement. If you think about it, all you really need is the will and drive to continue. You may give up momentarily, but you have the privilege to ask God for the grace and tenacity to begin again. It is important to get up after a setback, failure or disappointment, because God will meet you in motion. While God will comfort us when we are down, we can't stay there because He is expecting us to get back in motion toward the goal that is set before us. When we get moving again, God will meet us while we're in motion, and give us strength for the journey at hand. While we must have faith on this journey, we must be willing to put feet to our faith. James 2:26 Teaches us that faith without works is dead, and the great news is that God will bless your works. What are you believing God for today? This is what you should be working on, whether it's the startup money for a new business, the part in a theatrical production or starting a new family, God will meet you as you step out in faith-filled motion toward those goals. We must do more than sit and pray, we must act. Are you taking acting courses, seeking out auditions or saving money for your business venture? When God sees that you have enough faith to move out, He'll meet you in motion with favor and increase. Write the business plan, start the first chapter of the book, begin to clear your schedule for the new opportunities that will begin to pour in. While you are sitting back waiting on God to move, He's waiting on you to get up and move by faith, then He will meet you in motion.

DAY 37 PRAYER

Abba Father,
I know that faith without works is dead, so please awaken me today.
Help me to get up and go forth towards my dreams and goals. I
understand that I may experience setbacks, but please increase my faith

so I can begin again. I pray for great faith that will produce great works needed to get things done. I'm confident that you'll meet me while I'm in motion. Amen.

LEAN IN

It's important to get that prophetic push that comes from spending time in the presence of God, and coming out with clarity of purpose, direction and strategy. Now, it's time to walk out what God has given you to do. I've personally watched God meet me in the interview, while writing the book and while trying to faithfully pursue the things that He has put in my heart to do. So, my encouragement to you is this, the time to rise is now! Take the leap of faith and give God something to bless. Show God and the world what you're working on and working with. I promise you that He will meet you while you're in motion!

Day 38

Pandora's Box
Dedicated to Henry and Judith McGhee

Around the age of six years old I was given a yellow record player and a book with a record inserted in the front cover by my adoptive mom, Judith McGhee. She jokingly reminds me that I would ask her to go to the basement and play the record for me while I stayed safely at the top of the stairs to enjoy the story. The title of the story was "Pandora's Box", and I can still remember the narrator's warning to Pandora in the short story, "Don't Open the Box! Don't Open the Box! Whatever you do, don't open the Box!" was a bit scary! Those who are familiar with the Greek mythology know that Pandora's curiosity got the best of her. Well, she opened the box and all types of horrid things were unleashed into her world. I'm writing to caution you, just as the narrator of the story issued a warning to Pandora, please don't allow your curiosity to get the best of you. Curiosity can open your life up to some unnecessary pain, frustration and complications, as well. Many times, we are influenced to try things simply because the people around us are smoking, drinking or even using illegal drugs. We ended up playing a real dangerous game with experimentation. The things we experiment with can be exciting and fun in the beginning, but oftentimes, we later find that we don't like all of what was unleashed after we opened that box. The wrapping may have been pretty, but the contents of the package left a lot to be desired. What if the one time you decided to try sex, you lost your virginity and contracted a sexually transmitted disease that you cannot give back. I have a few friends that have experienced this, and they are longing for a do-over. If only they could go back in time and choose differently, they would be so elated. Some may have curiously experimented with drugs, but this experiment can leave you with a habit that you really can't afford to maintain. Don't let your curiosity get the best of you, 2 Corinthians 10:5 teaches us that we can cast down imaginations, because one wrong choice motivated by curiosity could drastically change your life forever. I am shouting to you, don't open the box, don't open the box, whatever you do... leave that box, the one you know isn't for you, closed and untampered with! Wait on the Lord! Be of good courage! All good and perfect gifts come from above. Wait on the package God has in store for you to arrive. It will be marked, "Destiny... Handle with Care!"

DAY 38 PRAYER

Abba Father,
You are a good Father. I can trust you to give me what I need. Help my curiosity and desires not to be focused on what I shouldn't have, but more on what will happen if I wait patiently for what you have prepared for me. Amen.

LEAN IN

We are given good advice from our grandmothers, mothers and aunties. They warn us that the stove is hot, that the knife is sharp and that this person isn't the one for you. We get all types of age-old wisdom that is passed down from generation to generation, but the problem is that it usually falls on deaf ears. You don't have to learn life lessons through hardship and suffering, you can learn by listening and applying principles from those that you perceive to be successful, and from those that you've watch fail miserably. The grass is not greener on the other side. Everything that glitters in not gold. Fat meat really is greasy. My adoptive father, Henry McGhee, used to always tell me that a hard head makes a soft behind. I am issuing a warning to you, sis: Don't open that box!

Day 39

Peep A Snake

No weapon that is formed against thee shall prosper; and every tongue that shall rise against thee in judgement thou shalt condemn. This is the heritage of the servants of the Lord, and their righteousness is of me, saith the Lord.
- Isaiah 54:17

One of the key things I teach my mentees is how to peep a snake. You might ask what that even means. Well, let me tell you. This is something that I learned as I was being developed in prayer and spiritual warfare. I have had experiences where God showed me things and people who were working against me, but through the Bible, in Isaiah 54:17, He encouraged me that no weapon formed against me will prosper. Although the weapons won't prosper, they still will form. 1 Peter 5:8 tells us that our adversary the devil roams about the earth seeking to cause harm to God's people. While we are moving in purpose we will run into active opposition from the adversary, but he is a spirit, so he embodies and uses people. If he shows up, it will more than likely be a sister, cousin, employer or even a friend. I have developed the ability to see enemy activity through those around me while staying poised, prayerful and powerful. We are not to stop and deal with every form of attack or enemy opposition, if so, the enemy would win. We'd be so distracted and perplexed that we wouldn't get anything done. Jesus identified his Judas. He acknowledged him, then carried on in purpose, what an example for productivity! Another reality is that many of our attackers are on assignment. They've come to cause us to press into prayer, become more determined to produce, and stay humble after producing. What you've got to do is Peep that snake! Identify clearly and acknowledge who and what you are up against. Then seek out the power of almighty God to help you bypass every trap they have set. Be confident in this and remember no weapon shall prosper!

DAY 39 PRAYER

Abba Father,
It is painful to have opposition. Especially when it shows up through those we love, or thought were truly on our team. I ask for the spiritual discernment to see all that's at work around me yet remain wise as a serpent and harmless as a dove. Amen.

LEAN IN

The greater the level, the greater the attack. The greater the increase, the greater the attack. We want the more of God, but we must know that we will have real serious opposition, due to our favor and success. It comes with the territory dear-heart. Use the pain of betrayal, gossip and lies to propel you deeper into prayer. It's the only place you can take that great pain. Somehow, I think that's the whole point, though. Haters give you a push and an edge. Don't be moved by everything you see. Peep a snake...remain poised, prayerful and powerful.

Day 40

People Lie!

Deception is an act or statement intended to make people believe something that is not true and is often used to get what the deceiver wants. Most of us have experienced deception at some point in our lives, whether through a childhood prank or maybe through a business deal gone bad. It is a terrible feeling to discover that someone has hidden the truth to take advantage of you. Although we have experienced fraudulent people or situations, we don't properly prepare those who come behind us for what could happen to them. We teach our children at a young age how to share, play nice and show love, but a balanced teaching would also include lessons on safeguarding their possessions while playing nicely because everybody doesn't always have the best intentions for them. Even our girls, at the appropriate age, need to be taught about young men who are, more than likely, after one thing. Do we share with our young gifted men about being mighty men of valor and men of their word? There is a new colloquialism we've been using that says, "stay woke", but the question is are we woke or on alert ourselves? Or are we so thirsty for love, money, fame and wealth that we close our eyes to what's in front of us just to believe a lie. I have personally lost valuable time in my life that I can never get back after dealing with people who turned out to be fraudulent and deceitful. I don't want you to be naïve. Be open to the fact that people lie. Jeremiah 17:9 says that the heart is deceitful above all things, and desperately wicked, and people will tell you exactly what you want to hear about your looks, product and merchandise to get what they want from you. Don't lose your life trying to gain love and don't waste years trying to get affirmation. Allow God to fill you with His love and cover you in your most vulnerable places. Proverbs 4:23 teaches us to guard our hearts with all diligence because out of it comes the issues of life. The process of recovery after dealing with fraud and deceit may take years, and that's just more time wasted.

DAY 40 PRAYER

Abba Father,
I know that the Holy Spirit is given to us to lead us into all truth, so
please order my footsteps away from those that are deceptive in nature.
Give me a greater measure of discernment needed to avoid being
repeatedly taken advantage of. Please break these types of vicious
cycles in my life. Amen.

LEAN IN

There is a term that is commonly used as it relates to dating. We
introduce our love interest as our friend. However, I am wondering if
that is the appropriate term to use. Many are often friend-zoned for years
with no real commitment made. We need to discern who our real friends
are in our interaction with love, business and ministry. I've personally
had promises whispered that sounded so sweet and sincere at the time,
only to find out that the person decided to change their mind. It is
devastating to be fooled, but you can recover. Fool me once shame on
you. Fool me twice... means a lack of prayer and judgement on all parts.
Let's ensure to never be deceived ever again.

Day 41

Pinch Me! I Must be Dreaming!

Anyone ever received a good old-fashioned butt whipping from the Lord? I have, and I truly advocate quick acknowledgement and repentance from sin that brought on God's correction in the first place. It seems like when God pulls out his spiritual belt, it is a long time before He puts it away. As I received my chastening from the Lord, I was reminded of Hebrews 12:6 where the scripture states that the Lord chastises whom He loves. Though I didn't like it, this is a good indication that I was a true child of God. God loved me enough to take the things from me that I worked hard to obtain but didn't need. He allowed me to reap the harvest of some of the negative things I'd previously sown. Some of my seasons of chastisement seem to last FOREVER. This was the case with God's children in Psalm 126. They were returning from a time of captivity that they brought upon themselves by being willfully disobedient. Although their chastising lasted for many years, it didn't last forever because God chose to turn things around for them. It had been so long that when it was time to be delivered from the chastisement, they felt like they were dreaming. God has a way of lifting the struggle and lightening the load right before our eyes, so much that we will feel like it's a dream. He won't stop there either. He will also fill our mouths with laughter, tongues with singing and we will again be able to testify of all the great things he is doing in our lives. Learn the lesson and never return to the things that led to your chastisement again.

DAY 41 PRAYER

Abba Father,
Help me be real enough to admit that all adversity is not brought on by the enemy. Help me to be spiritually mature enough to own up to my repeat offenses that caused my chastisement, and to never repeat them again. Amen.

LEAN IN

God told me to stop it. He sent warnings, but I was so weak and such the victim in my mind, that I just made many excuses. God decided to toughen me up through the process of chastisement which involved a stripping away of certain parts of me, to include some material blessings. Although I was a new Christian, God was teaching me early that He is merciful, and that there is a window for growth, but I still didn't have forever to rid my life of sin. A properly placed belt on my spiritual backside led me to some pain and tears. However, I stuck with God, endured my chastising season, and was made better by it. I am a stronger, disciplined Christian because of it. I am so glad to have been able to experience this truth. God is love. He is also the ultimate parent. He utilizes time out as well as the rod. It's true that the sooner you own your sin and repent, the sooner you'll head out of captivity and experience the freedom you've been dreaming about!

Day 42

Power of Accountability and Partnership

There is a familiar hymn I like entitled "Yield Not to Temptation". I really like these lines best: "Yield not to temptation for yielding is sin, each victory will help others to win; Just ask the savior to help you, to comfort, strengthen and keep you". My former pastor would always suggest that one would become perfected at doing whatever they practiced. When it comes to temptation, we must be self-aware. You have to know your kryptonite and not go through life as if you are a super hero with an impenetrable costume. I suggest that you know your own self and be true to that. Although temptation comes in many forms, there are so many in the kingdom who continue to fall into the sex trap. In 1 Corinthians 7:8-9, Paul recommends single-hood, but he suggested marriage if you're not able to keep your urges under control. Temptation is not always sensual in nature. I have a close friend who had a strong temptation with gambling. Life is a series of tests. Even Jesus was tempted. In Luke 4:13, the bible states that the tempter left tempting Jesus for a season. We will be presented with many opportunities to take the bait as well. Whatever the area of temptation, be fully aware that the tempter, the devil, is coming back. This juncture is what many of us miss when we think that a new title or age will somehow erase that place of temptation. Ecclesiastes 4:9 teaches us that two are better than one, so, I suggested setting up an accountability partnership to help you through your times of temptation. Pray for the right spiritual person to offer you wise counsel, encouragement and prayer to overcome temptation. Don't attempt to make it all alone.

DAY 42 PRAYER

Abba Father,
Everything lays bare before you. You know me. You know the areas that
I am weak. I ask you to send a strong spiritual accountability partner to
help me when I am most vulnerable and susceptible to failing. Amen.

LEAN IN

When counseling, I've often asked people to pinch themselves.
Afterwards, I remind them that they are FLESH and as long as they are
wrapped in flesh, they are susceptible to temptation. I don't care how
much you preach, pray or speak in tongues; you are still wrapped in
flesh. You will have to identify the areas that you are prone to fall or
fail. Failure to do so will set you up to be embarrassed by the adversary.
Pride does come before the fall. You can't set up covering and added
protective measures if you can't be honest with yourself and others. You
can live above temptation. Be real and be ready to partner with a strong
spiritual accountability partner.

Day 43

Pregnant Pause

You are a person designed by God with a specific purpose in mind. In order to effectively walk out that purpose, you must experience what I call a **"PREGNANT PAUSE."** This is when God orders your footsteps to a place of respite. God's plan is for you to be renewed. It is during this time of renewal that your passion comes back. This time of renewal is going to require that you pause. For example, when you sleep, the body works to repair itself from damages occurred that day. Also, your mind and spirit need regular breaks in order to reboot. If not, you will fizzle out. There is nothing worse than being in a working marriage or ministry relationship with someone who's lost their passion. They are merely going through the motions checking off a check-list and uninspired.

Let's talk about the pregnant pause. The pregnant pause is not a time to watch hours of reality TV or read your favorite magazine, although it may include those activities. A pregnant pause is a loaded, God-ordained and God-designed time of rest that has been ordered to fill and impregnate you with vitality, strength and instruction. It is during the pregnant pause in your life that God downloads your next steps, heals your damaged emotions after experiencing hurt or explains to you how to navigate through a difficult work experience. Psalm 40:1 says, *"I waited patiently for the Lord; and he inclined unto me, and heard my cry"*. You need to understand that there are God appointed times of stillness for the purpose of recovery and rebirth. Your waiting won't last forever. You will begin again. Take time out to embrace the pause. Allow God to fill you with wisdom, grace and understanding for your next chapter. If you accept the pause, you will be amazed at what God puts in your spiritual womb. He'll give you strength to carry to term and birth out what He has placed inside of you. What is being birthed is different for each of us. What are you birthing this season? Be still and allow God to reveal, during a pregnant pause, what he wants you to birth.

DAY 43 PRAYER

Abba Father,
I know that I am a part of your Kingdom and that I am chosen to be here,
but I get busy, and I need balance. Help me to hear your still small voice
calling me away to times of respite, refreshing and reconnecting with
you. Amen.

LEAN IN

I have a term that I call the "Prophetic Push." This is when you get
alone with God. During this alone time, God speaks instructions and
strategy to you. You will leave out of that place of respite pushed into
purpose. God has used this prophetic push to get me through my
marriage, ministry and employment season. There's no way to continue
with momentum and motivation without down time with Jesus Christ. It
is imperative to make time for a pregnant pause. God will fill you with
everything you need to achieve His desired results.

Day 44

Prioritize YOU!

I woke up this morning with intentions to write, but I bumped into a crisis that needed responding to before I could even get to my keyboard. The struggle was real! Even though life has a way of throwing obstacles at us, we all should have real intentions to lead a balanced life that includes making time for ourselves. I often encourage the ladies in my mentorship group to book themselves, meaning to slate time on their calendars to pursue their goals and dreams. I ask them questions like: What do you want in this season of your life? Are you prioritizing time for those things that are important to you? I shared with them that it is possible to look back five to ten years and discover that you have done a lot for other people, but nothing major for yourself. It would be a sad state of affairs to see growth, progress and increase in the lives of the people you've helped while failing to make any real progress with your own goals and dreams. Isn't this the story of many of our lives? We are helpers, nurturers, lovers, givers and birthers. We do this well. What we don't do well is pour an adequate amount of time and energy into ourselves. Why is that? I think the reason can be two-fold: first, we don't really know our own worth, and second, we are somehow getting something out of becoming a "Martyr for the Kingdom". Our dreams and goals must die a slow death as we help cultivate and nourish the dreams of others. This is not God, Sis! Visit the parable of the talents in Mathew 25:14-30. God gives to each person according to what He knows they are able to handle. I am suggesting that you do inventory to find what has been deposited inside of you. Afterwards, pencil YOU in! Prioritize you! As you get into prioritizing YOU, you'll start pursuing a life that is purposefully booked to capacity fulfilling your goals and dreams too.

DAY 44 PRAYER

Abba Father,
I am clear that you have given me gifts that should be used to serve
others. Help me receive the revelation that I can also use those same
gifts to help myself. You desire a return on what you've deposited within
me. I want you to be pleased with the time, energy and effort that I allot
to my own personal cultivation and development. Amen.

LEAN IN

How in the world do I make time for myself, you might ask? My answer
is that you prayerfully ask the Holy Spirit to show you. It has differed
for me over the years. I used to put the kids to bed early with a Disney
movie to carve out some time for myself. Moving forward, I'd utilize
the wee hours of the morning to exercise with my Zumba DVD before
work. Sometimes, pressure on the job pushed me to visit the university
library to read the Psalms. Now, the local coffee shop on Saturday
morning has become a great place for me to really focus on current
projects. It is imperative for you to find out what works for you. If not,
you'll always help others achieve their goals while missing out on what
you were intended to accomplish. Prioritize you!

Day 45

Purpose Attracts!

Purpose is one of your most attractive features. When you discover the purpose for which you were born, align yourself with that purpose and then begin to walk in it. The magnetism that is formed is so great that it will draw to you exactly what you need to fulfill it. Have you ever met a person that appears to have things just given to them? It seems they don't have to work hard, but things just fall in their lap. Well, this is a description of the new you, flowing and going in your purpose. When you truly dive into the purpose and plan God has for you, withholding nothing, you will begin to attract everything you need to fulfill your purpose. Since purpose is a magnet, and you're walking in it, you now have magnetic properties too. You will draw supplies and investors to you. Even the invitation for team members and staff will be sent forth without you putting forth the effort to secure them. Purpose has afforded you a new charisma that works like a charm. You'll find that people want to bless you and be good to you, so don't spend another day worrying about where the money, people and things you need are coming from. God knows what you need. Even more, Philippians 4:19 teaches us that God will supply all of our needs, but what he needs is for you to show up each day willing, able and committed to His cause. You will have what I call "defining moments." This is where God shows you things that are critical to fulfilling your destiny and purpose. Partner with the Holy Spirit through prayer, faith and confession to take hold of your next making it your now.

DAY 45 PRAYER

Abba Father,
You will provide everything that I need to fulfill my purpose. I don't have to struggle with questions like: "Will I ever marry?", "Where will I live", or "How will I pay for this or that?". I trust and believe that where you guide you provide. God continue to make me attractive as I

walk out my purpose so I can draw close to everything necessary to fulfill all that you've assigned to me to do. Amen.

LEAN IN

I can't stress this truth enough that if we walk out what God assigned to us, He will work out the logistics and make provision. He will order our steps and the steps of others to cause our paths to cross, just to make destiny happen. The world calls it luck, but we call it favor and divine connections. Get involved in your purpose and enjoy everything it will attract. Don't spend your life pursuing the ideal relationship, dream job or material things. Pursue God! You'll find those blessings chasing you down and overtaking you!

Day 46

Purpose, Process and Preparation

Thou therefore endure hardness, as a good soldier of Jesus Christ.
- 2 Timothy 2 :3

Being in purpose feels really good, but the process, not so much. Jeremiah 29:11 states that God thinks good thoughts towards you, but He also knows what it will take to get you to the fruition of those thoughts which contain your purpose. You won't always like the path that God chooses for you, in fact, sometimes it's hard to believe that a loving God would even order your footsteps through hardship, suffering and pain, but God knows it's for your making. He's making you into the person you need to be in order to fulfill your God-given destiny. Although there is no greater feeling than knowing you're right in the center of God's plan for your life, I strongly encourage you to do as 2 Timothy 2:3 says which is to endure hardness as a good soldier of Jesus Christ during your training days. You'll eventually make it through what I call pure preparation phases and stages. Once you are complete, He promises to perfect or mature that which concerns you. You'll be amazed at how much you've grown and how much better equipped you are for life. It's an amazing after-effect of processing, but fulfilled purpose is the ultimate reward.

DAY 46 PRAYER

Abba Father,
Thank you for revealing your purpose to me. Thanks for helping me understand that my process had purpose. Open my eyes to see the new person that I'm becoming as a result of my process. Amen.

LEAN IN

I was so low for many years because I did not understand God's processing. When I did gain the understanding that God was orchestrating things to further shape and mold me to fulfill my purpose, all I wanted to know was when it will be over. I grumbled and complained, but I also cooperated. God let me know while I was in process that there was greater ahead, so I moved through it. It took years and I don't have a desire to revisit my prior process at all, but I am grateful for every bit of it now. I can say with confidence and joy that I have been processed and prepared for my purpose. Rest in the fact that God knows what we need when we need it and our job is just to trust Him.

Day 47

Recycling Evil

If you have not figured it out by now, I am super-transparent. I open my heart and life in an effort to bring you behind the curtain of my life. It is my hope that by doing so, you will let me in to share God's love and wisdom with you.

I had a prophetic dream when I was away at basic military training that my biological mother died. I was not saved, and I didn't realize it was God preparing me for what was to come next. The dream was so real, and I was so upset that I woke up and shared it with my drill sergeants. Of course, they dismissed me, probably thinking I was merely homesick. The very next day the chaplain sent for me to tell me that my biological mother had died. I immediately made plans to go home to bury her. While home, I went to the apartment where she lived, and everything was still as it was after her suicide from the blood on the ceiling to the chair and chords she used. My goal for going there was to secure clothes for my younger sister, but I can remember blocking out what I saw that day until later. The next couple of days were a blur. I attended her funeral, made sure my baby sister was in a safe place and headed back to Fort Jackson, SC to resume my training. I'd missed my flight which put me back later than the time I was given and could have caused me military repercussions. When I finally returned, I ended up on the barracks bathroom floor screaming. I screamed until things went black. I started down a long black tunnel but somehow snapped out of it. I was examined by the army doctor and sent off with my military buddies to resume my training. Later, I heard a woman share her testimony of having a nervous breakdown and how it all started with her feeling like she was headed down a black tunnel. Just then I realized that even though I didn't really know God or attend church at that time, the hand of God was on me. It was Him who had kept my mind and snatched me back from going too far. More recently, I heard a lady share about having a nervous breakdown. She mentioned that it all started with her screaming uncontrollably. At that moment, if I ever had any doubt before, I didn't have any more doubt that God kept and spared me. I believe He brought me out so that I can share my stories and experiences with other women to build them. I call this recycling evil. I lost my biological mom due to substance abuse and ultimately mental illness. Instead of being victimized, I want to be used to help save other women. Women are often faced with so many obstacles, challenges and being mishandled, but, what if we all chose to recycle the bad things that were done to us? What would happen if we didn't allow what happened to us to further victimize us or limit us? What if we took things a step further and rescued other women that God allowed to cross our paths? Ultimately, everyone in your life's circle could win in life! Recycling pain often leads to purpose. There is a reason you survived what you walked through.

DAY 47 PRAYER

Abba Father,
Every single woman reading this book has a story, and so do I. Please help me to use my life's experiences for the good, so I can go from being a victim to victor and use my pain to help others. Show me where to start today. Amen.

LEAN IN

I cannot not go back to change anything in my past. I can only make a difference in my present. I have sought to understand the choices that my mom made and the things that happened to her that led to her ultimate demise, but I've come to peace with all of it. I do what I do now in honor of her memory. I make myself available to other women, and I take time with them. I am compassionate and try hard not to judge them. I've often told myself I can't go back in time to save my mom, but I can use my gifts and abilities to help others. I call this recycling evil. I use my brokenness to help the broken. You can choose to be better not bitter due to unfair disappointing things that have happened to you. Every time you allow God to use you to bring restoration, help and healing to someone, it's like giving the enemy a black eye! Recycle evil!

Day 48

Another Re-run and Repeat?

Have you ever watched an old movie on television that you weren't sure if you'd seen it before? You say to yourself... I think that I've seen this movie before. As characters and scenarios play out, you feel that you are almost positive, you've seen the movie before. However, the movie was so good, you continue to watch. You move further into the movie totally intrigued, confident you did see the movie before, but it's so good you can't stop watching it. I come to suggest to you that if you look around your life only to see the same movie scenes playing over and over, you may be experiencing a re-run. However, the plot may have twisted a bit, so you open up to familiar actors that appear phenomenal this time. Oftentimes, we re-enter familiar relationships, circumstances and scenarios outside of the counsel and leading of Holy Spirit. We enjoy the repeat performances as they play out because they offer a sense of excitement, extreme passion, and sometimes just much needed fun at first. Is it our need to orchestrate our destiny, time table, and outcome that causes us to ignore the fact that we've seen this play out before? We know what unfaithful looks like and we know that heartbreak shows up in the third scene. We should, because we had the leading role in this episode that has turned into a mini-series. Pay attention when you see similar scenarios resurface in your life. Stop fighting to make things "different this time around". It is exactly what it is. You don't want to look up having wasted days, months or even years trapped in an old re-run that is destined to end in the same painful way it did in the past. We must take our power back, turn the television off, and get into the presence of God. You have a date with destiny. God wants to give you something to look forward to. He'll guide you to something beautiful, something better and new! If you yield your life to the master, you will have a happy ending and a time of celebration. It takes real surrender to trust God to usher you out of the cycles of re-runs and repeats, and into your future, full of fresh new things that 1 Corinthians 2:9 assures us of.

DAY 48 PRAYER

Abba Father,
Help me recognize cycles and patterns on site. I don't have any more
time to waste. Amen.

LEAN IN

How many times are we going to date the same man in a different pair of
Jordans? How many dates are you going on with same type of woman
with a different color weave? Are you on the seventh interview?
 Visiting the 20th church? If so, go back and read this again from the
beginning!

Day 49

Return to Sender

In your patience possess ye your souls.
- Luke 21:19

I am about to take you to school. I'm going to share one of the most powerful lessons that I've learned over the years. It is that you don't have to take the bait of offense. You do not have to respond to people. You can actually choose to ignore their bad behavior and attempts to get under your skin and pull you out of character. I used to be all over the place responding to the actions of others, and what I was really doing was giving them the power to make or break my entire day. I was letting them change my entire mood. I was prepared to change ministries a couple of times and even switch jobs, but my hubby kept me anchored. I was ready to move at the slightest bit of discomfort caused by people. Now, how immature was I? God has taught me that I can choose whether or not to be offended, so I choose not! I've grown to the point that I don't do a lot of talking about haters. We all have them. They are in the shadows lurking and struggling with our success. Every now and then they will surface and make attempts to bring us down or throw us off our game. However, I made the choice not to take the bait, and you can do the same. They will irritate you, get under your skin and even make you want to visit your "before Christ" behaviors, but don't even give them the pleasure of seeing you respond. I remember driving home after having left church early because of someone else's disrespectful behavior, when I heard the spirit speak to me that they will continue to do what they do as long as they see they're getting a response. Really God? Really? Thanks for the tip. Now, no one gets a response. You could be right on the verge of resorting to physical violence, but stay poised, and send that negative energy right back in their direction! Don't let their hate and other toxic energy on board. It may be difficult at first, but you truly can learn to return all of that unwanted negative energy and the emotions that are attached to it, right back to the sender. It's OK to really be unbothered. In Luke 21:19, we are taught that we must possess our own soul, or emotions with patience. No one else should have that much influence over you to have control of your emotions. If you practice this principle enough you will truly become unbothered and any negative emotions that creep in will be fleeting. You hold the power over yourself. You decide what you let in. You make the choice to continue to have a great day by guarding your peace.

DAY 49 PRAYER

Abba Father,
Give me grace to deal with the difficult people in my life. Many are on assignment to throw me off the scene and hunt for my destiny, but with your help, I won't be detoured. Help me send all negativity back, in Jesus name. Amen.

LEAN IN

It is a very true statement that misery loves company. I suggest you RSVP- No. I will not be attending! Folks will see your light, your peace, your joy, your progress, your man, your style, your grace and it will bother them. It will bother them to the point that they set out to bother you. I am telling you to remain UNBOTHERED! Treat them just like a gnat, and shoo them away! Do not step outside of your purpose to even engage them. Listen to me, it's a distraction. Return to the sender!

DAY 50

SAVED GIRL MAGIC

Now faith is the substance of things hoped for, the evidence of things not seen.
- Hebrews 11:1

We've all heard the term "Black Girl Magic." It speaks to wonderful magical qualities found in women of color. I'd like to speak to the amazing abilities found in women (or men) of faith. I'll call it "Saved Girl" (or guy) Magic. What gives us that magical ability to do extraordinary things? What gives us that edge and power to achieve? Our secret weapon is our faith. Faith allows us to leap! It under-girds us through the grueling process of becoming. Our faith is our identity. We are faith girls. We faith It right into our next. Right into new dimensions. We continue to overcome hardship and tragedy by faith. Hebrews 11:1 teaches us that faith is the substance of things hoped for and the evidence of things not seen. In our hands, we hold concepts, ideas, projects, plans, and witty inventions that this world is yet to see. We take hold of it. We possess it by faith. In Romans 4, the bible teaches us that Abraham hoped against hope, considering not the deadness of his body, or Sarah's womb. We are inconsiderate girls. We choose not to consider what man suggests to us that cannot be done. We are fierce in our faith. Always moving faith forward.

DAY 50 PRAYER

Abba Father,
We know that everyone is given a measure of faith. Help us to build upon that faith. Help us to recognize that what we are walking through currently is a test of our faith to grow our faith. Amen.

LEAN IN

God woke me up at 6am to encourage someone with this. I think His desire for you is to embrace the power of faith. My husband was diagnosed with what the doctors say is an incurable disease four years ago. We have not allowed illness to stop us from doing anything God has given us to do. I grab ahold of what God says about my situation and move faith forward into my next. We walk by faith and not by sight. It's Saved Girl Magic!

Day 51

Sing A New Song

I truly believe that the Lord has a sense of humor. Every time I find myself complaining from a negative space, I feel a prompting to read Psalm 96. When I open the psalm and begin reading, I immediately chuckle, because this song is God's way of reminding me to curtail the murmuring and complaining. God was letting me know, with no uncertain terms, that I needed to discontinue my current chorus of murmuring and complaining, and that I was to sing unto Him a new song. What God was really saying was to take my complaints off of repeat. Have you ever found yourself stuck in a place where it seems the negative thoughts are on a repeated playlist in your mind and you find yourself rehearsing the problem or issue over and over again? Well, in reality, it is our responsibility to kick negative, stinking thinking out of our thought life. You wouldn't let any unclean, unsanitary thing in your home or car, so why do you allow stinking thinking to linger in your head? You have the right and responsibility to evict those nasty images and thoughts, immediately. It's not as difficult as it seems either. It could be something as simple as putting some uplifting, anointed praise music in your ears to combat the negative thoughts. Even though you may not feel it at first, keep it there. It will help you overcome the negativity in your space. Since we live in a fallen world, the worst of life can happen to the best of us on any given day, but we have to fight to stay in a positive place of faith. Also, you really need to identify what fills you up when you're spiritually empty. I find that I become negative when I am depleted both naturally and spiritually. You have to schedule fill-ups in order to stay away from murmuring and complaining, and to be able to continue singing the new song of faith and trust that God wants to hear from you.

DAY 51 PRAYER

Abba Father,
I don't want to sound like a broken record mentally and verbally
rehearsing everything that is wrong in my life. Help me to sing a new
song that identifies you as the great and majestic God who has the
ability to change my entire situation with just one word. Amen.

LEAN IN

When you've dealt with any type of abuse, or if the worst part of life seems to keep happening to you, like me, you probably have the ability to go to a negative place without much provocation at all. It seemed as if the smallest life issue could instantly send me into a defeated mindset. I finally matured and eventually disciplined myself to see God's hand at work even in the most disheartening situations. I do get off at times, because I'm human. Now, when I have negativity on repeat, God gently nudges me and whispers ever so softly in my ear, "It's time to sing a new song, I'm tired of your current playlist". Sing a new song of triumph and victory today!

Day 52

Sixty... Still A Secret?

Let's talk a little bit about Christian dating. You may ask what I could possibly know about Christian dating since I've been married for 26 years. Well, I have observed some things out here in these Kingdom streets and I have a few wisdom nuggets that I'd like to share. The first thing is, you should only approach dating when you truly know that you are worthy of love. This means you love you, first, flaws and all. If you head out into the world of romantic love affairs without first having received God's love, which leads to self-love, you may be in danger of placing your heart into the hands of someone not equipped to love you in the way you deserve to be loved. Second, I advise you, as I do my mentees to seek God concerning the seasons of life. For example, is this a season to date, or is this a season to focus on reaching your academic or career goals? God will give you the proper timing for everything in your life. Is it really that deep, you ask? Yes, it is that deep. I shared with one of my spiritual daughters that God wanted to do some very specific things in her life before she found true love. Sure enough, she scaled the corporate ladder to a top management position, raised her son to be an honor roll student and is now living in one of the nicest condos here in Baltimore County. Then, she re-entered the dating scene. I encourage my girls to allow him into the friend-zone for a season, meet him at the coffee house and have conversations to determine if you even like him. I have observed a desperation in some of the single ladies that I've encountered where every man they run across is potentially Boaz. You know Boaz, the wealthy distant relative who rescued and married Ruth after her husband, father-in-law, and brother-in-law had died in the book of Ruth 4:6. It seems as if their actions are mostly motivated by fear when I see them basically give up their bodies, credit, car, and so much more in attempts to hook Boaz in a relationship. Unfortunately, I've watched these attempts go up in flames many times. I tell my ladies, while you're in the coffee shop enjoying some good friend-zone time, be prayerful and attentive to hear what the Holy Spirit is speaking to you about him. He should be happy to be in your presence, and seeking God concerning you as well. When you approach dating from this perspective, you can exude confidence and be objective. Becoming sexual right away will throw all your objectivity out of the window and blind your eyes to a problem in his character that may be staring you in your face. It's so important to do it God's way so that you can hear clearly and avoid heartbreak. Lastly, do not give a man wifely treatment if he can't even take you to meet his family. I watch young women lay out the royal treatment for a man who won't even date them publicly. I issued a challenge to my spiritual daughters; I told them if he can't or won't post a picture with the two of you together on his social media and change his relationship status within 24 of hours of you asking while dating, delete and block him. If he can't make you public, you're a secret, sis. Don't allow any man to keep you as his dirty little secret texting you at midnight asking, "WYD?". You are nobody's secret. Go public, or boy, go home. You don't have to heed my advice or even accept the challenge I issued to my mentees. You may think that much of what I am saying is old and antiquated. I get that. However, I don't want you to look up to find yourself sixty, and still a secret.

DAY 52 PRAYER

Abba Father,
Show me my worth. Please help me see and understand that I'm not something to be hidden, and that I am one of your beautiful treasures to be shown off to the world. My dating life should not be done in the dark and shrouded with secrecy because I am a child of the light. Please, turn the light on for me, so I can walk in it. Amen.

LEAN IN

I have not been kept a secret, mostly because I have not been desperate to be loved. I think I feared rejection so much in my younger years, that I ran at the first sight of potential relational problems. I decided early on that I'd rather be alone than to pretend that I am really loved when I'm not. Why do we fear being alone? I do understand that loneliness can be painful, but so are toxic relationships. I encourage you to talk to Abba

Father about timing and what He has in store for you. When you hear from Him, it will dispel all your fears, and you can approach dating with confidence and contentment. I am praying for you today. I am not suggesting today's dating scene is easy. I just believe that God cares and wants to bless you in every single area of your life.

Day 53

Slap Me and I'll Slap You Back!

Bam! Right across my face with a spiral notebook book. "BOY! Are you crazy?!" Before I knew it, I was running across the room in full attack mode. I had just experience physical abuse at the hand of my high school boyfriend. I don't have the testimony that I allowed someone to continuously beat on me. Unfortunately, I do have to report the sad fact that I stayed in this toxic relationship after the assault. When I did try to leave, he would show back up in a harassing and threatening way. Because I was not the type of person to take a slap and not slap you back when I was younger, I asked two of my male cousins to go to his house and have a conversation with him. I didn't know how it was going to go, I simply told my family about the problem I was having. I didn't come from a church background and I knew my family would lay hands, but not the holy kind. They immediately went to have a meeting with my ex-boyfriend and their intent was not to pray. It was interesting to note that weak men who abuse and assault females tend to back down when confronted by a strong man. This same scenario played out again a little later in my life. I began to ask myself what was it about me that I was drawing the type of male that felt it was OK to abuse and assault females? I still don't have the answer, but I do believe that engaging in premarital activities with this type of male led him believe he had some level of ownership over me. Although I didn't know this then, there are so many issues, hurt and pain that could be avoided if we did things God's way. God's word and ways are always correct! I'm sure this passage won't be popular, but it's my truth. Abuse of any kind is never okay. Verbal abuse is just as bad. If you are reading this today and you're experiencing abuse of any kind, seek out help and support immediately. So many women, even in the church, suffer in silence. God did not design you to be a punching bag. You deserve so much more. Counseling is not a dirty word. Wise counsel coupled with prayer can help you get to the root of why you draw abusers and allow the abuse to continue. Proverbs 11:14 reminds us, *"Where no counsel is, the people fall: but in the multitude of counsellors there is safety"*.

DAY 53 PRAYER

Abba Father,
Touch the person reading this devotional. Help them identify abusive
people in their lives. Abuse comes in many forms, but it's not your design
or desire that we be continuously hurt in any manner. You are our help.
You are our way out. Show us the way! Amen.

LEAN IN

The person that struck me was first a trusted friend. We were friends
before dating, but I changed from friend to property in his mind. He felt
I was his property to do with whatever he pleased, but I am God's
property! You are God's property too! Abuse is often unreported
because the person experiencing the abuse is fearful and ashamed. It's
important that we are discerning and prayerful, especially when
mentoring or raising young ladies. We need to take time to educate and
prepare them for what's out there in the complicated world we live in.
My adoptive parents had no idea that I'd experienced that type of abuse
because I kept it to myself in fear and shame until I finally told my
cousins. Let's keep honest and open communication with our young
ladies and young men. We need to let them know that we are a safe
place to talk in the event that abuse is taking place. We must teach them
a little more than all the popular bible stories we learned as children. We
need to prepare them for life. Make sure those you love know that you
are an advocate and support system for them, and that there's no need to
be ashamed.

Day 54

Spousal Privilege

In Isaiah 54, God, through the prophet Isaiah is reaffirming his relationship with the church, and restating his constant and perpetual love for his bride after having chastened her. He offers the same covenant, peace and promise of greater prosperity to you today, because He is in covenant relationship with you too. When you are in a marriage relationship, you have what's called "spousal privileges". This means you have access to your spouse's income, pension and all benefits. In other words, you can wield their name, status, power and authority. One of the promises God made in Isaiah 54 was, though they were barren, they would bear more children than the married wife. What area in your life seems barren, and has little, to no production? Trust that God is going to make it up to you and begin to shift your mind to look to your other covenant benefits found in His word. Those promises that are found in His word are what He has in store for you. God is making His power, influence and authority available to you as part of your spousal package. Don't make the mistake of becoming bitter because you seem to be working at a disadvantage in some areas. You are in covenant with one who has every advantage and is making them available to you too.

DAY 54 PRAYER

Abba Father,
You told me that you are my husband, and you promised that the childless widow will have more than the married wife. Help me to rest in the fact that you are the real difference maker, and because we are in covenant, you are going to make things better for me. Thank you for every promise. Amen.

LEAN IN

This is one of my favorite passages of scripture. The truth is that the playing field is not even for everyone because there really are those that do not receive the same love, support and opportunities as others. However, the good news is that God sees all. He knows what we are working with and knows what we are lacking. You don't have to spend your life being bitter and in recovery because you didn't have a father present, the best education or best living arrangements growing up. I am a witness he'll make it up to you. God is the difference maker, and He is the answer to whatever you missed. Get into a good, strong relationship with Him and take advantage of those great spousal privileges.

Day 55

Styled by Grace

For by grace are ye saved through faith; and that not of yourselves: it is the gift of God.
-Ephesians 2:8-9

Be clothed with grace. Grace is God's unearned and undeserved favor. One way to clothe yourself with grace is to forgive yourself and stop trying to redeem yourself from your past. What do I mean by that? People often gain acceptance and love from others through actions or works, and as a result, attempt to gain God's acceptance and love by their works as well. They almost rationalize within themselves that if I can do enough good deeds, they will cancel out my prior bad behavior. Thankfully, there is good news, you do not have to attempt to redeem yourself from your past, because Christ already worked that out when he shed his blood at Calvary to atone for your sins. Ephesians 2:8-9 reminds us that we are saved by the gift of grace through faith, and not of ourselves. More importantly, not of works. Understand that you have permission to put on grace because you are forgiven, and through Jesus Christ, you are good enough.

Another facet of Grace is that it is a special God-given ability to do a specific task. God gives us an assignment, then extends the grace to complete it well. We all have been given at least one grace gift, but it's our job to identify it and work it to the best of our ability, by the grace of God. You even have the privilege to ask God for His grace to do the everyday tasks that have been assigned to you. God can extend grace to be a parent, to run that office, and to raise that autistic child at your request. There is grace available to help you do whatever needs to be done. God's grace can change your tasks from arduous to easy at your request.

DAY 55 PRAYER

Abba Father,
Help me to receive your gift of grace today. I want to be clothed with
grace and accessorized with your special enablement, so I can complete
what you've assigned for me to do and make you proud. Amen.

LEAN IN

Wife, you have a grace to love your husband. Mother, you have specific
grace to raise your children. Supervisor, God has given you the grace to
build and lead your team. There is absolutely no need to try and do it in
your own strength. Ask God for a daily dose of grace to make things
easier for you. His yoke is easy, and His burden is light. Be fully clothed
in His grace!

Day 56

Testing Tips

God's promotion process includes testing. You want to go higher? Experience increase? Want more exposure? If you answered yes, get ready for the test. Testing reveals your readiness or lack thereof. In many places around the country, graduation is called a "promotion ceremony". Take a minute and think back. How many tests did you have to take and sometimes retake before you met graduation or promotion requirements? So, it is in the natural... it is in the spirit. I call a testing environment, God's lab. It's important that you recognize that life is not simply "happening to you". You have been surrounded by a predetermined set of circumstances uniquely designed to vet and qualify you. It is major because your release is at stake. There is no set of tests you'll experience that is not common to others. In other words, everyone is going through some type of spiritual development. Everyone has spent or will spend time in God's lab. Be careful of falling into feelings of isolation and self-pity. It's the enemy's job to make you feel like you're the only one suffering or going through. You are in great company and should have a sense of pride that God found you test worthy. Be excited that He wants to get something greater to you than what you currently have. The wrong perspective will have you wandering around the wilderness for forty years, like the Children of Israel in the book of Exodus, when it should've only been an eleven-day trip. It's even evident in the life of Joseph, in the book of Genesis, where he spent quite a bit of time in God's lab. Promotion, honor and status will not come without a cost. Pay your dues then pass your test. Show God that you're ready for promotion.

DAY 56 PRAYER

Abba Father,
Many only want to experience you in the good times, but I also need to know you as Rabbi, my master teacher. You know how to test me to bring out the very best in me in any circumstance. Give me proper

perspective and the ability to pull on the wisdom that you've already placed within me to pass each test that I face. Amen.

LEAN IN

I jokingly call myself "Josephina", after the Bible character, Joseph. I have experienced several promotions both in the church and marketplace, and a season of testing proceeded each one. I did not understand God's process at first. I was full of self-pity and would complain. It felt like a dark cloud was over my head and bad things always happened to me. Until I got into the face of God and He began to teach me how to employ principles that I learned through spending time with Him. Principles like submission to authority, showing unconditional love, praying for my enemies and honoring my spouse. When I came to understand that the circumstance was merely a test, I stopped thinking it strange when the fiery trial hit my life. I also began to expect that promotion was right around the corner, contingent upon me passing the test. You should expect it too.

Day 57

The Hunted

Mean words and heavy hands left me self-loathing and cutting my wrists. I believe that Satan hunts us down while we are children. I think he's studied mankind, our family heritage, and birth conditions enough to know when he sees greatness. The Bible states that the enemy comes to kill, steal and destroy. He stalks from the onset. He's vigilant in his effort to stop us before we ever get started. He can't rob us of the God-given talents and abilities that have been placed inside of us. He can't lift the mantle or stop the mandate that has been commissioned by God. What he can do is operate in the circumstances surrounding us. He relentlessly sends out his blood hounds to trace those connected to us. He influences them to damage, maim and silence us. What methods does he use? Molestation, verbal abuse, and family favoritism, just to name a few. He wants us to be so fragile, tattered and inwardly mangled that there's no way our amazing gifts can emerge from such a being. What he fails to realize is that we are also protected and passionately pursed by God. He's been relentless in pursuit to protect and provide for us. Despite the bumps and bruises along our path to destiny, we will emerge greatly. We will be emotionally and physically healed by the one who created us. We'll emerge more than conquerors and overcomers.... survivors.

DAY 57 PRAYER

Abba Father,
I can remember asking you "why?". You responded with what you didn't allow to happen. You blocked the enemy's hand from doing what would've destroyed me. What was allowed only delayed me. I am thankful for all that you've healed and made whole. It's complete. Amen.

LEAN IN

I remember asking God why He allowed certain things to happen to me. I know many may read this and think I am a bit crazy. I'll dare to share anyway. God's response to my question was an open vision. He took me back to the time and season of abuse. He showed me what was allowed. He also showed me demonic activity all around me operating in folks that meant to further harm me. God blocked it. It is my assumption that what was allowed was for me to use what I've experienced to help many people. We should not blame God. We should seek God to understand then walk out the purpose in it. This is what makes you more than simply a survivor. This makes you more than a conqueror. This makes you an overcomer! You can now hunt what once hunted you. Helping other victims become like you.

Day 58

The Secret is in The Sauce

I joke with my mentees telling them that the secret is in the sauce. You make an honest attempt to recreate Big Mamma's potato salad. You do your best by adding all of the normal ingredients that one would add to the dish, but you can't seem to get the same outcome or taste that Big Mamma so fabulously delivered each time. "What's missing?" you might ask? Well, you've heard it said, "The secret is in the sauce". What is it that Big Mamma adds that makes it taste so good? What is it that's keeping that sister's marriage going strong for 20 plus years? How has sister girl finished earning her bachelor's degree and is now working towards her master's degree? How is that single mom who raised those boys alone able to see all of them grow to do amazing things? I need to know what's in that sauce. I need to know what I am missing that's caused me to miss out on yet another promotion. Talk to me! Share the age-old recipe. I want to know what it takes. Well, it takes mentorship and having a teachable spirit, as the old mothers in the church would say. It will take being humble and open enough to be educated on a few things. It takes coming to the realization that with all of my intellect and professional training, I still have some areas that I need mentorship in. Do you have teachers? Mentors? Trainers? Do you have a Big Mamma who's willing to share? If not, I suggest you get one, quick. Some things aren't taught, but they are caught by being in the presence of and serving awesome kingdom women and men. The one single ingredient added to my sauce is service. My husband and I have learned to stay close to and serve our spiritual leadership throughout the duration of our marriage. In addition, I try to serve with excellence in my home, church and marketplace. I don't care if it's a secular situation, I approach it with the mindset of a servant. Matthew 23:11 teaches us that the greatest among you is a servant. Being in this posture has afforded me the ability to stick to tasks, stay in place and continue connections to people that I wouldn't have otherwise endured. I know we live in a time where everyone wants to be a boss and be recognized or known as important. The best kept secret is when you serve others and then Jehovah goes to work to ensure that you are prepared. Service is what's lacking, in many cases. A lack of service will keep your life bland and tasteless. It can't be all about the title on the door, the car you drive and whatever else you floss. If all the effort you exert is for you, your life will not pop and be fulfilling. When you pour yourself into serving others, your life experience becomes meaningful and full of zesty mouthwatering delicious flavor.

DAY 58 PRAYER

Abba Father,
Help me to embrace your methodology of service. While the world's system suggests that we grind, hustle and focus on getting what is due us, you set the example of serving people while here on earth. Please help me to understand and experience the power and importance of service. Amen.

LEAN IN

I hope the secret ingredients shared will help you to not only make it through adverse circumstances, but also afford you a few tips and tools needed for you to experience an abundant life. I shared with my mentees how I've served my husband, my pastor and unsaved bosses, and watched God open door after door for me because I remained in the posture of service. Use your unique skills and talents to serve and refresh your leaders, family and those in the community around you. You will receive favor and honor as a result. It won't always feel like this posture is working like you think it should, but stay the course and watch Jehovah elevate you in due season! One of the main secret ingredients in the sauce is definitely service. Many miss it! Don't miss out on the pure power, productivity, and prosperity that service unleashes!

Day 59

To Be Continued…

Is this ever going to end? Will my marriage ever get better? I am wondering if this difficult child will change? My question to you is, what if it doesn't change? Will you stop? Will you leave the relationship? Will Junior be put up for adoption? I want to talk today about continuing when there is no apparent change in sight. People don't usually talk about what to do on day number 2,753 of living with your situation. How do you keep going when you see nothing? You hear nothing. There's no movement. You feel no hope for change. If you tell the truth, you don't really like the husband, church or kid anymore and you have literally made a mental list of all of the reasons to justify leaving. How do you continue when you feel numb, unengaged, and there is no motivation to pray or apply faith to the situation? Here's what you do: You live beyond your current feelings! Faith is not based on a feeling. Obedience is not based on a feeling. Agape love isn't even based on a feeling. You continue even when all hope and faith are lost. I can recall some of my Genesis 18:21 moments when I laughed just like Sarah. I have looked right in the face of situations and laughed as I whispered to God, "no way". I actually chuckled, and told God... There is no way you could fix this. I also suggested to God... Let's just throw the whole situation away and move on to the next one. Sometimes you will feel like there's no hope for love, passion or care to return to a failing situation. Can I submit to you that just because you're at the end of your patience for a situation, God is more than likely just getting started? I think God often waits for us to get to our breaking point and we're exhausted with attempting to make things happen through our own efforts. He longs to show you how he can bring life and resuscitate your dying situations. Have you secretly given up on a relationship, child or ministry? I encourage you to hand it over to the one who can bring it back to life. Do not quit, your miracle is to be continued!

DAY 59 PRAYER

Abba Father,
Someone is feeling numb today. They have checked out of the process
due to hurtful and disappointing situations. We need your hand to hold,
stabilize and revive us. Amen.

LEAN IN

My husband and I married at ages 21 and 22. We were both young, spoiled and very selfish. It wasn't long into the marriage that we both determined that we did not like each other very much. It's very possible to love someone while not liking their actions towards you. I found myself going through the motions of marriage. I would honor my husband's position as head of my home, but my service was dry, and full of underlying resentment. Of course, God met me in motion (my dry attempt to be a dutiful wife) and encouraged me to lay down all unforgiveness, resentment and pain. My response to God was, "okay, but I doubt very seriously if my change in heart will make a difference at all", and I kind of scoffed at God's instructions. I am so glad that God's ways are not my ways, and that His ways are higher than mine. My obedience unlocked and unleashed God's ability to change my marriage and our hearts towards each other. I hope my story encourages you to stay and fight! It's not over until God says it's over! You'll be amazed when God turns it around for you. Your miracle is to be continued!

Day 60

Twice Punished! I don't think so!

And be ye kind one to another, tenderhearted, forgiving one another,
even as God for Christ's sake hath forgiven you.
-Ephesians 4:32

Forgiveness is a very powerful tool given to us. Ephesians 4:32 teaches us that we must forgive one another, as God has forgiven us. Forgiveness is a gift that you give to yourself as well. The act of forgiving releases you from the control that the offender held over your life. You are not required to stay in close relationship with those that continue to hurt you over and over again. It is okay to forgive them and love them from afar. You can pray for those who mean to harm you from a distance. If the perpetrator is a spouse or co-worker, or an individual that you must deal with daily and cannot put distance between you, there are ways to be in close proximity and create distance at the same time. I am around people that would seek to say and do things to challenge the resolve of my forgiveness on a daily basis but my block and ignore strategy is too strong. I have learned how to guard my heart. I can love you while still loving and protecting myself too. It's called self-protection. While ministering and caring for others, we are put in positions to be hurt, and normally hurt people will hurt people! Once you know the potential to be hurt is there, you must move in wisdom.

DAY 60 PRAYER

Abba Father,
Help me to forgive. I bring my hurt and brokenness to you. Please
begin the process of healing that only you can facilitate in my life. I look
to you and trust you with my wounds. Please make me whole. Amen.

LEAN IN

I have a thing that I do called "Get In and Get Out"! I have become masterful at identifying the jealous, envious and the petty. We are people of faith, but we should not be naive. It's okay to have your eyes wide open and accept the fact that everybody is not for you. The Holy Spirit will also reveal problematic spaces and places. God does not desire you to be the martyr for the cause always lending yourself to people to take a perpetual beat down. Pump your breaks! No repeat offenses. Place a little safe distance between the cruel hearted and your heart.

Day 61

Who Will Go After a Better Thing?

I would like to suggest that there's nothing wrong with being spiritually ambitious. Once we move past the initial fear surrounding the call that God has for our lives, we should mature to a place where we have some positive ambition. I think we should want to attain every level that God has in store for us. I'd like to know who will go after a better thing? Anyone want more of God? Psalm 24 teaches us that it involves ascension. We must go up to meet Him where He is. Oftentimes, we want God to come to us. He does meet us at the point of our need, but he wants us to aggressively go after all that He has for us, and we should reach a point in our spiritual walk where we are spiritually ambitious enough to do just that. There is a slogan from today's civil rights movement that suggests that we "stay woke", and I want to echo that slogan in this devotional. I am suggesting that all the spiritual sleepy heads wake up to your possibilities and stay woke! Be a God-seeker! A God-chaser! Have you ever thought that God wants you to run a network, own your own school or foster a home for children? Be determined to go for it. Join with me in seeking the mind of God to find out more of God. I bet there is more in store than we realize. Don't settle for being average. Don't go for the status quo. Go after a better thing!

DAY 61 PRAYER

Abba Father,
I need you to restore my passion to pursue you. My secret struggles of my flesh and impurity have dulled my desire to pursue. I know you have more for me. I don't want to miss it. Amen.

LEAN IN

There is no need for false humility. You have a spiritual portion and inheritance waiting for you. Yes, you! Despite your habits and past hang-ups, He knows you fully and still wants you to experience his fullness. So, let's go! Go for it spiritually. Don't allow someone else to come collect what was handpicked and set aside for you. Desire, set your mind and go after a better thing!

Day 62

Wifey Resume

Are you single? Do you want to be married? I recommend using this alone time to build your wifey resume. What is a wifey resume? It's something I created to help the ladies that I mentor prepare themselves for marriage.

Here are a few points to consider as you develop your own wifey resume:

1. Marriage is job. A job that includes a title change, job description and list of duties. When you take on this new title, you are signing up to assist your husband in fulfilling his purpose. This is the role of the help meet. In Genesis 2:21, God gave Adam a help meet that was suitable for him. Are you suitable for a man?

2. Marriage requires a specific skill set. You can start to build those skills as you walk out your own purpose and operate in service to others. These skills have less to do with focusing on your external than they do your internal. While externals are important, no real man wants a woman that only has a beautiful outer shell but is underdeveloped in other areas of her life. Do you want a man who's merely biceps and triceps with no real intellect? You should want him to be complex and interesting. A man wants the same from his wife.

   Let's take a look at some of the skills that I think you'll need before arriving at the altar:

   • **Spirituality** - Wives are often the very backbone of the family. There are times that you'll find yourself holding everyone up in prayer, offering encouragement and oftentimes, a word from the Lord. A woman that prays for her man and family is a woman that helps him protect the family unit. You must be more than cute. You must be skilled in spiritual warfare as well. The meaning of the word help meet is to see the enemy afar off. Can you see, Sis? We have to be more than cute. We have to be keen, sharp and experienced.

- **Purposeful** - Plan to approach marriage with a sense of identity. Of course, you need to find your identity in Christ, but what else does God have slated for you? Use this time of singleness to work on your career path, discover your spiritual track, and find yourself serving in a church so you can discover the many gifts God has placed within you. Everything you develop while serving will transfer over when you serve your husband and family. Yes, I said serve. He'll serve you with his particular skill set as well. Marriage is absolutely a team sport, so allow God to refine you and make you the best teammate there is.

- **Substance** - I have encountered a few shallow sisters whose sole focus is to secure a great man. If you're going to gain the attention of one of God's great men, you too must be great. You may be able to use a properly fit bodycon dress and stilettos to get him, but you will need more substantial things like agape, kindness, endurance, wisdom and faith to keep him. There are a lot of women with external beauty out there, but you should stand out as a rarity who has beauty, brains and spiritual substance. God knows how to help you become substantive so that you can be a tremendous help to your future husband.

DAY 62 PRAYER

Abba Father,
There are ladies who are low and lonely because their relationship status still hasn't changed from single to married yet. Please fill them with pure joy today and reassure them that like David said in Psalm 31:15, their times are in your hands and that you make everything beautiful at the right time. Amen.

LEAN IN

Your singleness is not a curse. Everything you are experiencing right now is building you into a future wife. I had no idea that my future mate would be a pastor. Who grows up thinking they will marry a minister? I will tell you that was not on my schedule, in fact, that thought was furthest from my mind. I can look back over my life to see how certain experiences, both good and bad, shaped me to be the woman that my husband needs me to be in order to help him walk out his purpose. Thus, fulfilling God's call for me to be his help meet. I have my own purpose which includes my career, being a mom and minister. I never lose sight of God's employ because he called me to be a help meet. I allowed Him to make me suitable. I have skills listed on my wifey resume. I can counsel, encourage, and develop our family's budget. I can pray down fire when the enemy comes for my man. I am more than lips, hips and fingertips. There are more skills required than what is performed in the bedroom. Your future husband will need to pull on your unique set of gifts. Use this time to work on building your wifey resume. Build you!

Day 63

Yo, where is Simon?

I need for someone to go locate my Simon right about NOW! As I was counseling a sister via text one morning, God gave me a revelation on the spot that truly blessed my entire life and blessed her as well. It was short, but profound at the time: Even Jesus was unable to carry his cross the entire time as he headed to Calvary to fulfill his purpose. There was a man named Simon from Cyrene, in Mathew 27, who was compelled by the Roman soldiers to bear or carry the cross for Jesus. We tell folks to pick up their cross, which symbolizes their specific set of heavy burdens or drama that's unique to their spiritual journey and follow Christ. What happens when that burden gets a little too heavy to bear? We tell folks that God won't put more on us than we can bear. Well, if that's the case, why did Jesus lay down His cross? Why did He need Simon? I am suggesting that there will be some periods in your Christian journey where you will indeed stop, put down your cross momentarily, and have to seek out some much-needed assistance. This may come in the form of a pastor, church mother, neighbor or Christian accountability partner. You don't have to be strong all of the time. You will at some point become spiritually depleted with no hope. I truly believe God allows this to teach us interdependence. We are the body of Christ fitly joined together. We each need what the other has inside of them to offer. God will set systems in place to ensure that we learn to love and embrace one another. He knows how to remind you that you can't make it on your own and cause you to actively search for help from your Simon.

DAY 63 PRAYER

Abba Father,
I am broken. I have come to the realization that there will be times that I'll feel like I'm drowning and I'm in need of rescue. I realize that I need a Simon. Please assign and send me a Simon today. Send someone to help me complete my spiritual assignment and fulfill my destiny. Amen.

LEAN IN

My younger sister, Musa, is my Simon. As I watched a movie recently, God revealed to me how great a help she's been to me over the years through watching a character in the movie. It was clear to me that I might not be here doing what I am doing today, nor would my family be in tact the way it is without her assistance. I always knew she was a blessing, but I didn't grasp the greatness of her influence until recently. God will reveal those that He has put in place to help you with purpose. You are not doing it on your own. If you need someone, ask God!

DAY 64

You are Under Arrest!

You've probably heard it said that you can run, but you can't hide. Are you a runner attempting to outrun the plan of God for your life? Do you know deep inside that God desires to have a relationship with you? Or maybe you are in Relationship with God but aren't ready to fully embrace the kingdom assignment God has for you. Well, your running days are over, because you are now under arrest by God's Love! God wants to take you, in the fullness of His love, to a place where you'll live a full and abundant life in Him. You may feel that surrendering your life wholly over to the Lord will restrict you from living your best life because the call of God may not line up with the course that you've charted out for your success. In reality, embracing the life God designed for you is the ultimate measure of true success. God designed you with a specific plan in mind. You have been given a grace gift, and a part in God's plan. Isn't it amazing to know that you've been included? You're written into the script. You don't have to figure life out all on your own. You serve a God that is invested in your success. Allow His love to arrest you today. Surrender your plans over to Him. Allow Him to meet you right where you are today. In the Message bible, Ephesians 3 assures us that God can do anything. You know far more than you could ever imagine, guess or request in your wildest dreams! He does it not by pushing us around, but by working His spirit deeply and gently within us.

DAY 64 PRAYER

Abba Father,
Thank you for always loving me. You've loved me from the beginning of my life, and you will continue to love and guide me. Amen.

LEAN IN

I woke up with a Jonathan McReynolds' song in my spirit. It is entitled, "Lovin' Me". I didn't grow up hearing terms like: God's calling, purpose, or destiny. I simply lived life. I tried to figure out life on my own terms not fully understanding that God had a plan. God loved me enough to show me the very reason that I was born, and He wants to do the same for you. Life is so much more fulfilling when you understand the "whys" of life! Surrendering your life to God's plan for you will cause you to live a life of abundant peace and joy that you could never secure on your own. Allow His love to arrest you today. He wants in!

Day 65

Are You Numb Enough?

I can remember going to my favorite fast food eatery as a teenager. I'd order a number four, then afterwards, I would consume even more food and include dessert. I can remember gorging myself with so much food that I would run to the parking lot to vomit it back up immediately afterwards. It wasn't long before I'd find myself repeating the same addictive cycle. I didn't realize it at the time, but I was using food to numb the pain I felt. It doesn't matter what caused the pain, the thing I want to point out is that I developed methods to cope with it. We all do it. Your numbing agent of choice may not be a fast food sandwich, maybe you fill the emotional void with overspending on your department store credit card. Sorrowfully, some are using prescription pills, alcohol or other illegal substances. Many men and women even use pornography or multiple sexual partners as a way to escape their personal pain. I believe that some people experience so much emotional pain and torment that they would reach for just about anything to numb it. God asks the question in Jeremiah 8:22, Is there no balm in Gilead; is there no physician there? Why then, is the health of the daughter of my people not recovered? Of course, the answer to that question is that Jesus is the balm and physician in Gilead. It is God's desire that we prosper and stay in good health even as our soul prospers. God is totally interested in healing your soul, mind and emotions. You can come to Him with any type of ailment. He is Jehovah Rapha, our healer. I am tired of merely coping, aren't you? I am ready to thrive. It's time to put away those things that we're reaching for that keep us propped up and barely making it and begin to seek God for wholeness. Are you struggling with addictive behaviors? God has healing and deliverance for you, when you are finally numb enough.

DAY 65 PRAYER

Abba Father,
Help me search for addictive patterns and behaviors in my life. Order
my footsteps to the path that you have laid out for me to experience
healing, deliverance and freedom in my life. Amen.

LEAN IN

We all reach for things to comfort us. What starts out as an additional
piece of sweet potato pie to soothe our hearts could end up being a full-
blown food addiction. I made a decision that I want to thrive. I want to
heal from the pain of my past, break destructive cycles and help others
find freedom. It's okay to look for habits and hang ups in your life that
are causing you to be limited or miss out on God's best. God is not
intimidated by your current struggle, but He wants to extend his mercy
and grace to you today to be free indeed!

Made in the USA
Coppell, TX
13 August 2022

81408913R00083